P9-CJQ-671

Marian
Gems

DAILY WISDOM ON OUR LADY

Donald H. Calloway, MIC

Available from:
Marian Helpers Center
Stockbridge, MA 01263

Prayerline: 1-800-804-3823
Orderline: 1-800-462-7426
Websites: www.fathercalloway.com
www.marian.org

Imprimi Potest:
Very Rev. Kazimierz Chwalek, MIC
Provincial Superior
The Blessed Virgin Mary, Mother of Mercy Province
Congregation of Marian Fathers of the Immaculate Conception of the B.V.M.
March 25, 2014
Solemnity of the Annunciation

ISBN: 978-1-59614-305-0
Cover Photo taken by Ileana E. Salazar, M.A. in San Ysidro, CA
Design by Kathy Szpak
Editing and Proofreading: David Came, Andrew Leeco, and Chris Sparks

Acknowledgments: Marian Fathers of the Immaculate Conception,
Mr. & Mrs. Donald and LaChita Calloway,
Mr. & Mrs. Matthew and Teresa Calloway,
Ileana E. Salazar, M.A.,
Teresa de Jesus Macias, Milanka Lachman, L.H.S.

Printed in the United States of America

MARIAN PRESS
STOCKBRIDGE MA 01263

To St. Philomena:
My Little Princess and Protector

Through the intercession
of St. Philomena,
may Jesus purify your heart
and keep you safe.

Blessed are the pure
of heart, for they
shall see God.
– Matthew 5:8

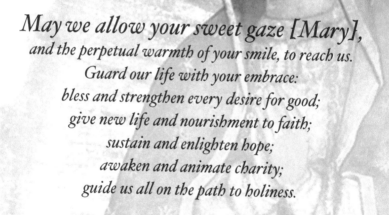

May we allow your sweet gaze [Mary],
and the perpetual warmth of your smile, to reach us.
Guard our life with your embrace:
bless and strengthen every desire for good;
give new life and nourishment to faith;
sustain and enlighten hope;
awaken and animate charity;
guide us all on the path to holiness.

– Pope Francis, Act of Entrustment to Mary,
October 13, 2013

On September 8, 2013, during the *Angelus* message at St. Peter's Square in Rome, Pope Francis made the following statement: "Jesus is the Sun, Mary is the dawn that heralds his rising." Don't you just love such simple statements as this! I sure do. It's short and pithy but theologically profound. Such pithy little gems of wisdom invite us to meditate and reflect upon their deeper implications for our spiritual life and journey. Indeed, ever since my conversion to Catholicism, I've always been amazed at how Popes and Saints have the uncanny ability of putting deep and profound Christian truths into just a few sentences. And as is evidenced above in the little gem from Pope Francis, I believe this is particularly true when it comes to Our Lady.

As a matter of fact, when I was a seminarian, I began collecting as many gems on Our Lady as I could find. I loved to use them as part of my daily meditation and prayer before the Blessed Sacrament. Yet, outside of my own personal love for them, I was never quite sure what else I would be able to do with them. Well, Divine Providence had a plan for these little gems, a plan that would bring them to others! In 2013, I published a book about Our Lady titled *Under the Mantle:*

Marian Thoughts from a 21st Century Priest, and in that book, I was able to include all of my favorite Marian gems at the end of each chapter. I really believe they added so much to that book, and many people who have read that book have told me that they absolutely loved the Marian gems sections. Many of them even encouraged me to put them all together in a separate book and call it *Marian Gems.*

I thought putting such a book together was a really good idea, but wasn't exactly sure how to go about organizing it. But guess what? Divine Providence once again showed me the way. One day, as I was thinking of a way to organize all the Marian gems into a separate book, I decided to count them and see exactly how many I had. I was completely startled when the number added up to 365! Incredible! A different quote for each day of the year! Perfect! And since Pope Francis was elected right after I published *Under the Mantle: Marian Thoughts from a 21st Century Priest,* I could now include his wisdom on Our Lady in the Marian gems book in the Introduction and for the February 29th date that shows up in leap years! 366 Marian gems. Perfect!

As you will note, the collection of Marian gems you find in this book are only from Saints, Blesseds, Venerables, Servants of God, and Popes. The reason for this is because these are guaranteed sources of Catholic wisdom in regards to Our Lady. Others, Catholics and non-Catholics alike, have made profound statements about God's created masterpiece, Mary, but nobody sums up the mystery of Mary better and with more authority than God's Vicar on earth (the Pope) and those we consider to be holy and worthy of our imitation (the Saints).

As you make your way through this book, it is important to note that though there is no particular reason for the order in which the Marian gems appear, I have intentionally tried, to the best of my ability, to match up a saint's liturgical feast day with something they said about Our Lady. Sometimes this worked, sometimes it didn't, but for those who are familiar with particular saints' feast days, you will quickly catch on to this as you read each daily gem. Also, I tried to have a particular Marian gem be appropriate for the more universally celebrated Marian solemnities and feast days in the Church. In addition, you will notice that under each Marian gem, there is a title of Our Lady provided, invoking Mary under that title and asking her to pray for us. Almost all of the titles that are provided are from various litanies to Our Lady used in Catholic devotional practices, but since I needed 366 titles, I have also extracted from the Marian gems themselves various titles in order to call upon Our Lady by using the very words of Popes and Saints.

Lastly, as you read *Marian Gems*, it might be tempting to skip around or jump ahead and read a whole bunch of gems in one sitting, but I highly suggest that you only read one Marian gem a day, meditating and pondering the deeper dimensions of what it means for you and your relationship with Jesus, Mary, and the Church. By following this method you will truly spend an entire year with Our Lady and fall more in love with Jesus and his Church, all through Mary. And if you would like to go deeper and unpack the theological depths and context of the Marian gems, please consider obtaining a copy of my Marian book *Under the Mantle: Marian Thoughts from a 21st Century Priest* (see the back of this book for ordering information).

I pray this little book is a great blessing to you and helps you spend a little bit of your day with Mary!

Fr. Donald Calloway, MIC, STL
Vicar Provincial
The Blessed Virgin Mary, Mother of Mercy Province

JANUARY

January 1

Behold, "the Mother of Jesus," Mother immaculate, Mother untouched, Mother who never experienced the pains of motherhood, Mother uncorrupt, Mother not deprived of the virtue of virginal chastity. She is spotless, a fitting Mother for the spotless Lamb.

– St. Albert the Great

Mother of God, pray for us!

January 2

All true children of God have God for their father and Mary for their mother; anyone who does not have Mary for his mother, does not have God for his father.

– St. Louis de Montfort

Our Spiritual Mother, pray for us!

January 3

As one cannot go to a statue of a mother holding a child and cut away the mother without destroying the child, so neither can one have Jesus without his Mother. Could you claim as a friend one who, every time he came into your home, refused to speak to your mother or treated her with cold indifference? Jesus cannot feel pleased with those who never give recognition to or show respect for his Mother. Coldness to his Mother is certainly not the best way to keep warm a friendship with him. The unkindest cut of all would be to say that she who is the Mother of our Lord is unworthy of being our Mother.

– VENERABLE FULTON J. SHEEN

Mother of my Lord, pray for us!

January 4

She is the Mother of the Life from whom all men take life: in giving birth to this life herself, she has somehow given rebirth to all those who have lived it. Only one was begotten, but we have all been reborn.

– BLESSED GUERRIC OF IGNY

Mother of Life, pray for us!

January 5

The life of Jesus Christ in us originates through
baptism and faith, thus we are conceived
of the Holy Spirit. But, like the Savior,
we must be born of the Virgin Mary.

– BLESSED WILLIAM JOSEPH CHAMINADE

Mother of God's Children, pray for us!

January 6

The Wise Men found our Lord in the arms
of his Mother. So did the shepherds.
This is not a coincidence;
it is symbolic.

– SERVANT OF GOD (FR.) JOSEPH KENTENICH

Seat of Wisdom, pray for us!

January 7

So submissive was he to her care that the door that slammed in her face in Bethlehem also slammed on him. If there was no room for her in the inn, then there was no room for him. As she was the ciborium before he was born, so she was his monstrance after Bethlehem. To her fell the happy lot of exposing, in the chapel of a stable, the "Blessed Sacrament," the body, blood, soul, and divinity of Jesus Christ. She enthroned him for adoration before Wise Men and shepherds, before the very simple and the very learned.

– VENERABLE FULTON J. SHEEN

Monstrance of God, pray for us!

January 8

God willed that his Son come into this world by being born of the seed of Adam and of a daughter of Adam that we might have the God-man for our brother and the Mother of God for our mother. Thus we have the same father and the same mother as the Son of God himself. We are his brothers, and as he is our mediator with his Father, so his heavenly Mother is a mediatrix between himself and us.

– ST. JOHN EUDES

Mediatrix, pray for us!

January 9

Because of a food, we were cast out of the loveliness of paradise, but by means of another food we have been restored to the joys of paradise. Eve ate the food by which she condemned us to the hunger of an eternal fast. Mary brought forth the food that opened for us the entrance to the banquet of heaven.

– St. Peter Damian

Mother of the Living Bread, pray for us!

January 10

If anyone does not wish to have Mary Immaculate for his Mother, he will not have Christ for his Brother.

– St. Maximilian Kolbe

Mother Most Amiable, pray for us!

January 11

For so great is her dignity, so great her favor before God, that whosoever in his need will not have recourse to her is trying to fly without wings.

– POPE LEO XIII

Dove of Simplicity, pray for us!

January 12

Our Lady's love is like a limpid stream that has its source in the Eternal Fountains, quenches the thirst of all, can never be drained, and ever flows back to its Source.

– BLESSED MARGUERITE BOURGEOYS

Life-Giving Spring, pray for us!

January 13

The Flesh born of Mary, coming from the Holy
Spirit, is Bread descended from heaven.

– St. Hilary of Poitiers

Mother of our Bread, pray for us!

January 14

O my Lady, my ruler, you who rule me, Mother of
my Lord, Handmaid of your Son, Mother of the
world's Maker, I pray you, I beg you, I beseech you,
that I may have the spirit of my Redeemer, that I may
truly and worthily know you, that I may speak truly
and worthily about you, that I may say whatever true
and worthy thing needs to be said about you.

– St. Ildephonsus of Toledo

Sovereign Lady, pray for us!

January 15

We shall never be able to love Mary as her Son loves her. For this reason, we can love her and desire to love her without measure, knowing that we shall never love her enough.

– SERVANT OF GOD MOTHER AUXILIA DE LA CRUZ
Our Lady of Banneux, pray for us!

January 16

When an artist has completed his masterpiece, he can do no more than to reproduce it in all its forms; when a genius has spoken the final word of his wisdom, nothing remains for him but to develop and explain it. When a soul has pronounced the unsurpassable word of love, she can do nothing more than repeat it in all its tones and with all the accents of that sovereign word. Similarly, after God wrought the supreme marvel of the Incarnation, he does nothing more in the world of grace than reproduce it, although it may be with faint and imperfect imitations of the masterpiece of his omnipotence and his love. The best likeness of Jesus' grace of union is Mary's motherhood. On account of this extraordinary grace, Mary is above every other creature, touching, as she does, the order of the hypostatic union.

– SERVANT OF GOD ARCHBISHOP LUIS M. MARTINEZ
Masterpiece of God, pray for us!

January 17

The Mother of God is the Ladder of Heaven. God came down by this ladder that men might, by Mary, climb up to him in heaven.

– St. Fulgentius

Ladder of Heaven, pray for us!

January 18

Love the Immaculate One with all your being, will and heart, but should you sense a time of aridity coming upon you and cannot awaken sentiments of love, do not worry much, for it does not belong to the essence of love. As long as your will desires only her will, then be at peace, for truly, then, do you love her, and through her, you love Jesus and the Father.

– St. Maximilian Kolbe

Immaculata, pray for us!

January 19

One cannot contemplate Mary without being attracted by Christ, and one cannot look at Christ without immediately perceiving the presence of Mary.

– POPE BENEDICT XVI

Mirror of Perfection, pray for us!

January 20

Where Mary is present, grace abounds and people are healed both in body and soul.

– ST. JOHN PAUL II

Health of the Sick, pray for us!

January 21

I wish to love the Mother of God as God himself loved her and still loves her. Imagine the boundless confidence God himself had in entrusting his only Son to her. And she remained ever faithful.

– St. Vincent Pallotti

Our Lady of Confidence, pray for us!

January 22

All periods of the Church's history are marked with the struggles and glorious triumphs of the august Mary. Ever since the Lord put enmity between her and the serpent, she has constantly overcome the world and hell. All the heresies, the Church tells us, have been vanquished by the Blessed Virgin, and little by little she has reduced them to the silence of death.

– Blessed William Joseph Chaminade

Mother of the Unborn, pray for us!

January 23

I am your servant [Mary], because your Son is my Lord. Therefore, you are my mistress, because you are the handmaid of my Lord. Therefore, I am the servant of the handmaid of the Lord, because you, my mistress, became the Mother of my Lord.

– St. Ildephonsus of Toledo

Mistress of the Heavens, pray for us!

January 24

O what an honor for us to do battle under this valiant captainess!

– St. Francis de Sales

Valiant Captainess, pray for us!

January 25

If Paul by his care and heartfelt tenderness gives birth
to his children again and again till Christ be formed
in them, how much more so does Mary!

– BLESSED GUERRIC OF IGNY

Tender Mother, pray for us!

January 26

True devotion to Christ demands true devotion to Mary.

– ST. POPE PIUS X

Virgin Most Venerable, pray for us!

January 27

Most holy Virgin, obtain for me from your Son this grace:
That I may love you more and more, trust you ever more
firmly, and treasure more dearly your glorious protection.

– BLESSED GEORGE MATULAITIS

Model of Trust, pray for us!

January 28

Just as sailors are directed to port by means of a star
of the sea, so Christians are directed by
means of Mary to glory.

– St. Thomas Aquinas

Star of the Sea, pray for us!

January 29

She [Mary] is a ship of treasures, bringing
to the poor the riches of heaven.

– St. Ephrem the Syrian

Ship of Treasures, pray for us!

January 30

She [Mary] is the ark of the true Noah,
to save the human race.

– St. John Eudes

Ark of the true Noah, pray for us!

January 31

We find ourselves in this earth as in a
tempestuous sea, in a desert, in a vale of tears.
Now then, Mary is the Star of the Sea, the
solace of our desert, the light that guides
us towards Heaven.

– St. John Bosco

Ocean of Love, pray for us!

FEBRUARY

February 1

Take away the sun that illumines the world, and the day is gone. Take away Mary, the Star of the Sea of the great, wide ocean: What then is left, but deepest darkness, the shadows of death, and impenetrable midnight?

– ST. BERNARD OF CLAIRVAUX

Fountain of Life and Light, pray for us!

February 2

If devotion to the Blessed Virgin is necessary for all men simply to work out their salvation, it is even more necessary for those who are called to a special perfection. I do not believe that anyone can acquire intimate union with our Lord and perfect fidelity to the Holy Spirit without a very close union with the most Blessed Virgin and an absolute dependence on her support.

– ST. LOUIS DE MONTFORT

Mother of the Consecrated Life, pray for us!

February 3

The Son whom she brought forth is he whom God placed as the firstborn among many brethren, namely, the faithful, in whose birth and education she cooperates with a maternal love.

– VATICAN COUNCIL II (*LUMEN GENTIUM*)

Mother of the Church, pray for us!

February 4

In every situation I will trustingly adhere to the Blessed Mother and go hand in hand and heart in heart with her to our Savior and to the Father.

– SERVANT OF GOD (FR.) JOSEPH KENTENICH

Mother Thrice Admirable, pray for us!

February 5

If the place occupied by Mary has been essential to the equilibrium of the faith, today it is urgent, as in few other epochs of Church history, to rediscover that place. It is necessary to go back to Mary if we want to return to that "truth about Jesus Christ," "truth about the Church," and "truth about man."

– POPE BENEDICT XVI

Pillar of Faith, pray for us!

February 6

She [Mary] is the woman long ago promised by God to crush the head of the old serpent with the foot of her strength. The serpent has been lying in ambush, employing every sort of stratagem to attack her heel, but to no avail. Alone she has crushed all heretical crookedness.

– ST. BERNARD OF CLAIRVAUX

Conqueror of all Heresies, pray for us!

February 7

Under her guidance, under her patronage, under her kindness and protection, nothing is to be feared; nothing is hopeless. Because, while bearing toward us a truly motherly affection and having in her care the work of our salvation, she is solicitous about the whole human race. And since she has been appointed by God to be the Queen of heaven and earth, and is exalted above all the choirs of angels and saints, and even stands at the right hand of her only-begotten Son, Jesus Christ our Lord, she presents our petitions in a most efficacious manner. What she asks, she obtains. Her pleas can never be unheard.

– Blessed Pope Pius IX

Intercessor for Fallen Mankind, pray for us!

February 8

A deep veneration of Mary removes the bitterness and harshness usually connected with the striving for perfection.

– Servant of God (Fr.) Joseph Kentenich

Comforter of the Afflicted, pray for us!

February 9

The reason why Mary became his mother and why he did not come sooner was that she alone, and no creature before her or after her, was the pure Vessel of Grace, promised by God to mankind as the Mother of the Incarnate Word, by the merits of whose Passion mankind was to be redeemed from its guilt. The Blessed Virgin was the one and only pure blossom of the human race, flowering in the fullness of time.

– BLESSED ANNE CATHERINE EMMERICH

Vessel of Grace, pray for us!

February 10

Mary is the glory of creation, the delight of the angels, the model of saints, the strength of the vacillating, the consolation of the weak and the secure refuge of sinners.

– SERVANT OF GOD MOTHER AUXILIA DE LA CRUZ

Our Lady of Refuge, pray for us!

February 11

Let us count as synonymous the expressions
saint and child of Mary!

– BLESSED WILLIAM JOSEPH CHAMINADE

Our Lady of Lourdes, pray for us!

February 12

Through her, as through a pure crystal, your mercy was
passed on to us. Through her, man became pleasing to God;
through her, streams of grace flowed down upon us.

– ST. FAUSTINA KOWALSKA

Mediatrix of Mercy, pray for us!

February 13

She [Mary] is the motherly principle, the apparition
of God's arm of mercy which even a person
with an icy heart has difficulty to resist.

– SERVANT OF GOD (FR.) JOSEPH KENTENICH

Apparition of God's Arm of Mercy, pray for us!

February 14

O holy Mother of God, remember us, I say, who
make our boast in you, and who in august hymns
celebrate your memory, which will ever live,
and never fade away.

– ST. METHODIUS OF PHILIPPI

Holy Mother of God, pray for us!

February 15

We are like ivy, which cannot support itself, but which, if it twines round a tree, can grow to great heights. Our souls, which also need support, grow rapidly in perfection if they trust the Mother of Mercy. We see this in the many saints who made rapid progress by loving and honoring her.

– BLESSED MICHAEL SOPOCKO

Mother of Mercy, pray for us!

February 16

She [Mary] desires to form her Only-begotten in all her sons by adoption.

– BLESSED GUERRIC OF IGNY

Spiritual Mother, pray for us!

February 17

God, who gave us Jesus Christ, wills that all graces
that have been, that are, and will be dispensed to men
to the end of the world through the merits of Jesus
Christ, should be dispensed by the hands and
through the intercession of Mary.

– St. Alphonsus Liguori

Dispentrix of Grace, pray for us!

February 18

Those who have great devotion to Mary not
only will be saved but also will, through her
intercession, become great saints.

– St. Vincent Pallotti

Prototype of Creaturely Holiness, pray for us!

February 19

To both Jesus and Mary, there are treasures in
darkness — one in the darkness of a woman,
the other in the darkness of a hill. Only those
who walk in darkness ever see the stars.

– VENERABLE FULTON J. SHEEN

Our Lady of Lichen, pray for us!

February 20

She [Mary] is his mystic channel; she is his aqueduct,
through which he makes his mercies
flow gently and abundantly.

– ST. LOUIS DE MONTFORT

Aqueduct of Mercy, pray for us!

February 21

From her own womb's immaculate flesh she gave
birth to the nutriment of our souls.

– ST. PETER DAMIAN

Lover of the Eucharist, pray for us!

February 22

Mary will be the happy bond to draw together, with
strong yet gentle constraint, all who love Christ, no
matter where they may be, to form a nation of brothers
yielding obedience to the Vicar of Christ on earth,
the Roman Pontiff, their common Father.

– POPE LEO XIII

Delight of the Papacy, pray for us!

February 23

No grace comes from heaven to earth but what
passes through Mary's hands.

– St. Bernardine of Siena

Our Lady of Grace, pray for us!

February 24

Love for Our Lady is the
driving force of catholicity.

– Pope Benedict XVI

Strength of the Faithful, pray for us!

February 25

When we have handled something fragrant, our hands
perfume whatever we touch; let but our prayers pass
through the hands of the Blessed Virgin,
and she will give them fragrance.

– ST. JOHN VIANNEY

Mother Most Pure, pray for us!

February 26

I love Our Lord with all my heart. But he wants me
to love Our Lady in a special way and to go to
him with my hand in Mary's.

– VENERABLE TERESA OF JESUS QUEVEDO

Vessel of Honor, pray for us!

February 27

Love Mary! … She is loveable, faithful, constant.
She will never let herself be outdone in love.

– ST. GABRIEL POSSENTI

Virgin Most Faithful, pray for us!

February 28

God has willed that we should have nothing that
would not pass through the hands of Mary.

– ST. BERNARD OF CLAIRVAUX

Aqueduct of Grace, pray for us!

February 29

Our Lady is the custodian
of our salvation.

– POPE FRANCIS

Custodian of our Salvation, pray for us!

MARCH

March 1

To no one is mercy granted except
through you [Mary].

– St. Germanus of Constantinople

Minister of Mercy, pray for us!

March 2

Heaven and earth will pass away before
Mary would abandon a soul.

– Blessed Henry Suso

Mother of Divine Hope, pray for us!

March 3

Noah's ark was a true figure of Mary; for as in it all kinds of beasts were saved, so under the mantle of Mary all sinners, who by their vices and sensuality are already like beasts, find refuge.

– St. Alphonsus Ligouri

Refuge of Sinners, pray for us!

March 4

The ark saved Noah and his family from the deluge; Mary saved the human race through Jesus Christ. Noah's Ark floated on the same water in which the world was drowning; Mary was untouched by the slimy waters of concupiscence and sin. Those who took refuge in Noah's Ark were rescued from death; those who take refuge in Mary do not drown in the flood of the passions. The earth was repopulated by those who had taken refuge in the Ark; Heaven is inhabited by Mary's faithful servants.

– Blessed James Alberione

Vessel of Divinity, pray for us!

March 5

Blessed, indeed, are those Christians who bind themselves faithfully and completely to her as to a secure anchor! The violent storms of the world will not make them founder or carry away their heavenly riches. Blessed are those who enter into her as into another Noah's ark!

– St. Louis de Montfort

Ark of Salvation, pray for us!

March 6

Noah's ark was a type of Mary. As, by its means, men were preserved from the Flood, so are we all saved by Mary from the shipwreck of sin.

– St. Bernard of Clairvaux

Singular Vessel of Devotion, pray for us!

March 7

After Christ, Mary is the greatest of God's blessings
sent to the Church, the gift of gifts beyond our
comprehension, because she can do all things
for us with God.

– St. Lawrence of Brindisi

Virgin Most Powerful, pray for us!

March 8

Let us then, whoever we may be, bless forever the
divine goodness which gave us Mary as our Mother,
our spiritual nurse, and our mediatrix.

– Blessed William Joseph Chaminade

Spiritual Nurse, pray for us!

March 9

Mary places herself between her Son and mankind in
the reality of their wants, needs and sufferings.
She puts herself "in the middle," that is to say she
acts as a mediatrix not as an outsider.

– St. John Paul II

Maternal Mediatrix, pray for us!

March 10

The apostle Paul exhorts those who want to obtain
grace that they should approach the throne of grace;
in other words, the glorious Virgin.

– St. Bonaventure

Throne of Grace, pray for us!

March 11

On Mary's motherly face Christians recognize a most
particular expression of the merciful love of God, who
with the mediation of a maternal presence has us better
understand the Father's own care and goodness.
Mary appears as the one who attracts sinners and reveals
to them, with her sympathy and her indulgence,
the divine offer of reconciliation.

– ST. JOHN PAUL II

Mother of Reconciliation, pray for us!

March 12

In your hands [Mary] are laid the
treasures of God's mercy.

– ST. PETER DAMIAN

Virgin Most Merciful, pray for us!

March 13

Through the Mother we have access to the Son, and through the Son to the Father. With such guides to lead us, let us have no fear at all of being refused reconciliation.

– St. Albert the Great

Queen of Confessors, pray for us!

March 14

There is no fruit of grace in the history of salvation that does not have as its necessary instrument the mediation of Our Lady.

– Pope Benedict XVI

Depository of All Graces, pray for us!

March 15

If you invoke the Blessed Virgin when you are tempted, she will come at once to your help, and Satan will leave you.

– St. John Vianney

Queen of Heaven, pray for us!

March 16

She has given us so many proofs
that she cares for us like a Mother.

– ST. THERESE OF LISIEUX

Lovely Mother, pray for us!

March 17

If our strength fails us, let us cling to the Mother of
Mercy, and hide, with childlike love, under the cloak
which she draws round us with a motherly gesture.

– BLESSED MICHAEL SOPOCKO

Mother Inviolate, pray for us!

March 18

If Mary and Martha's tears compelled Christ to raise their dead brother from the tomb, what sin can be so strong, that the power of Divine Mercy cannot extinguish it through the intercession of the Virgin Mother?

– ST. ANSELM OF LUCCA

Royal Highness, pray for us!

March 19

Mary is the depository of all graces, but who can better induce her to open the celestial treasury than Joseph, her glorious spouse? A servant of Mary will therefore have a tender devotion to St. Joseph, and by his pious homage of respect and love, will endeavor to merit the protection of this great saint. He will beg of him the grace of dying as he himself did, with the kiss of Jesus and in the arms of Mary.

– BLESSED WILLIAM JOSEPH CHAMINADE

Spouse of St. Joseph, pray for us!

March 20

The moment of conversion is not the same for all. St. Augustine, St. Mary of Egypt and many others spent a considerable part of their lives far from God, while others were ravished by grace from the very beginning. But however we are converted, the Mother of Mercy is always the instrumental cause, for, by God's will, no grace is given to us but through the mediation of the Immaculate Heart of Mary. Let us not be too certain that we are safe now and have no need of our Mother's care. Like little children we should always remain under her mantle, to press continually to the bosom of our Mother who nurses and rears us and obtains mercy for us.

– BLESSED MICHAEL SOPOCKO

Vessel of Mercy, pray for us!

March 21

She [Mary] is the "Administrator of Mercy" because
God has endowed her with extraordinary goodness,
meekness, generosity and kindness, with unparalleled
power, that she may desire and be capable of helping,
protecting, sustaining and comforting all the
afflicted, the miserable, and those who have
recourse to her in their needs and necessities.

– St. John Eudes

Administrator of Mercy, pray for us!

March 22

As flies are driven away by a great fire, so were the
evil spirits driven away by her [Mary's]
ardent love for God.

– St. Bernardine of Siena

Lover of the Trinity, pray for us!

March 23

Sanctity grows in the measure that we venerate Mary.

– ST. PETER FABER

Temple of God, pray for us!

March 24

Mary calls herself *ancilla Domini*, the handmaid of the Lord. Not to be this for any woman lowers her dignity. Woman's unhappiest moments are when she is unable to give; her most hellish moments are when she refuses to give.

– VENERABLE FULTON J. SHEEN

Handmaid of the Lord, pray for us!

March 25

"Full of grace" … is Mary's most beautiful name, the name God himself gave to her to indicate that she has always been and will always be the beloved, the elect, the one chosen to welcome the most precious gift, Jesus: "the incarnate love of God."

– POPE BENEDICT XVI

Full of Grace, pray for us!

March 26

There is nothing Mary has that is for herself alone — not even her Son. Before he is born, her son belongs to others. No sooner does she have the Divine Host within herself than she rises from the Communion rail of Nazareth to visit the aged [Elizabeth] and to make her young.

– VENERABLE FULTON J. SHEEN

Joy of Mothers, pray for us!

March 27

Jesus is Head of the Mystical Body of which we become members through baptism. If Jesus was born of Mary, all those who are part of Jesus must be born spiritually of her.

– BLESSED MICHAEL SOPOCKO

Mother of the Mystical Body, pray for us!

March 28

The ancient Fathers rightly taught that the Church prolongs in the sacrament of Baptism the virginal motherhood of Mary.

– VENERABLE POPE PAUL VI

Queen of Patriarchs, pray for us!

March 29

For the faithful can do nothing more fruitful and salutary than to win for themselves the most powerful patronage of the Immaculate Virgin, so that by this most sweet Mother, there may be opened to them all the treasures of the divine Redemption, and so they may have life, and have it more abundantly. Did not the Lord will that we have everything through Mary?

– ST. POPE JOHN XXIII

Sweetest Heart of Mary, pray for us!

March 30

To give worthy praise to the Lord's mercy, we unite ourselves with your Immaculate Mother, for then our hymn will be more pleasing to you, because she is chosen from among men and angels.

– St. Faustina Kowalska

Immaculate Mother, pray for us!

March 31

God rules the world and distributes his mercy through secondary causes, the principal one of which is the Mother of Mercy.

– Blessed Michael Sopocko

Reparatrix, pray for us!

April 1

Through her [Mary], the long warfare waged with the Creator has been ended. Through her, the reconciliation between us and him was ratified. Grace and peace were granted us, so that men and angels are united in the same choir, and we, who had been deserving of disdain, have become sons of God. From her we have harvested the grape of life; from her we have cultivated the seed of immortality. For our sake she became Mediatrix of all blessings; in her God became man, and man became God.

– St. John Damascene

Mediatrix of All Blessings, pray for us!

April 2

If we want to be Christians, we have to be Marian.

– Venerable Pope Paul VI

Model of the True Faith, pray for us!

April 3

Mary is powerful against heresy. Heresy is obstinacy in error regarding matters of faith. Mary is a hammer against heresy itself, but she is salvation for separated brethren of good will.

— BLESSED JAMES ALBERIONE

Our Lady of Walsingham, pray for us!

April 4

Every gift, every grace, every good that we have and that we receive continually, we receive through Mary. If Mary did not exist, neither would we, nor would the world.

— ST. LAWRENCE OF BRINDISI

Queen of the Cosmos, pray for us!

April 5

God is called Lord, and he wishes Mary to be called Lady. He is universal Lord of all things, and he wills her to be sovereign Lady of the universe. He is "King of kings and Lord of lords," and she is the queen of queens and sovereign of sovereigns.

– ST. JOHN EUDES

Lady of Nazareth, pray for us!

April 6

If you do not understand Our Lady, you do not understand Christianity, because Christianity puts her in a most extraordinary position.

– SERVANT OF GOD FRANK DUFF

Mother of the New Covenant, pray for us!

April 7

Never be afraid of loving the Blessed Virgin too much. You can never love her more than Jesus did.

– St. Maximilian Kolbe

Mother of Our Savior, pray for us!

April 8

The world will be completely Christianized if Mary will be known, imitated and invoked throughout the world.

– Blessed James Alberione

Mother of the New Evangelization, pray for us!

April 9

Every objection against devotion to Mary grows in the soil of an imperfect belief in the Son. It is a historical fact that, as the world lost the Mother, it also lost the Son. It may well be that, as the world returns to love of Mary, it will also return to a belief in the divinity of Christ.

– Venerable Fulton J. Sheen

Mother of Jesus, pray for us!

April 10

When will souls breathe Mary
as the body breathes air?

– St. Louis de Montfort

Our Life, Our Sweetness, and Our Hope, pray for us!

April 11

Oh, what great sorrow it must have been for the Mother, after Jesus was born, to think that they had to then crucify him! What pangs she must have always had in her heart! How many sighs she must have made, and how many times she must have wept! Yet she never complained.

– St. Gemma Galgani

Suffering Mother, pray for us!

April 12

Mary is the one who has the deepest knowledge of the mystery of God's mercy.

– St. John Paul II

Most Knowledgeable of God's Mercy, pray for us!

April 13

Full of kindness and mercy, he [God] has given over to her [Mary] in a certain sense the dominion over his mercy while reserving for himself the final day of judgment.

– SERVANT OF GOD (FR.) JOSEPH KENTENICH

Empress of Mercy, pray for us!

April 14

Among the effects of divine mercy we must enumerate three principal realities, which in turn embody numberless effects. The first is the Incarnation of the God-man; the second, his Mystical Body, namely Holy Church; the third is the Mother of the God-man, namely the most Blessed Virgin Mary. These constitute three admirable masterpieces of divine mercy.

– ST. JOHN EUDES

Masterpiece of Divine Mercy, pray for us!

April 15

Mary is the one who obtained mercy in a particular
and exceptional way, as no other person has.

– ST. JOHN PAUL II

Maiden of Mercy, pray for us!

April 16

Dearest Mother, how happy was my soul those
heavenly moments when I gazed upon you.
How I love to remember those sweet moments
spent in your presence, your eyes filled
with kindness and mercy for us!

– ST. BERNADETTE SOUBIROUS

Dearest Mother, pray for us!

April 17

Queen and Mother of Mercy. And this most loving
Mary has so completely won the heart of God's
mercy that he has given her the key to all his treasures
and made her absolute mistress of them.

– ST. JOHN EUDES

Mistress of Mercy, pray for us!

April 18

Every grace by which Jesus raises us to a supernatural
life passes through the hands of Mary.

– BLESSED ILDEFONSO SCHUSTER

August Mediatrix, pray for us!

April 19

She [Mary] knew her office and her mission: she accomplished these most faithfully, even to the very end, by cooperating with the Son as Coredemptrix. She prepared the Host for sacrifice.

– BLESSED JAMES ALBERIONE

Co-Victim with Christ, pray for us!

April 20

She is called the Queen of Mercy because she opens the abyss and treasure of divine mercy to whom she chooses, when she chooses and as she chooses.

– ST. BERNARD OF CLAIRVAUX

Queen of Mercy, pray for us!

April 21

It was fitting that this Virgin should shine with a purity
so great that, except for God, no greater purity
could be conceived.

– St. Anselm of Canterbury

Immaculate Mary, pray for us!

April 22

If we have a box in which we keep our money, we know that
one thing we must always give attention to is the key; we never
think that the key is the money, but we know that without the
key we cannot get our money. Our Blessed Mother is like the
key. Without her we can never get to Our Lord, because he
came through her. She is not to be compared to Our Lord, for
she is a creature and he is the Creator. But if we lose her, we
cannot get him. That is why we pay so much attention to
her; without her we could never understand how that
bridge was built between heaven and earth.

– Venerable Fulton J. Sheen

Tower of Ivory, pray for us!

April 23

Just as God preserved the blessed angels from sin through his Son, so you, O Beauty of Purity, will save wretched men from sin through your Son. For just as the Son of God is the happiness of the just, even so your Son, O Salvation of Fruitfulness, is the reconciliation of sinners.

– ST. ANSELM OF CANTERBURY

Beauty of Purity, pray for us!

April 24

Devotion to our Lord Jesus Christ and devotion to Mary are intimately united. The more we love Jesus Christ in the Blessed Sacrament, the more we love the Blessed Virgin; and the more we love the Blessed Virgin, the more we love the Blessed Sacrament.

– ST. MARY EUPHRASIA PELLETIER

Lover of the Blessed Sacrament, pray for us!

April 25

Are you afraid to approach God the Son? He is your
brother and your flesh, tempted in all things except
sin, that he might show you mercy. Mary gave you
this brother. But perhaps you fear the divine majesty
within him, because, even though he was made man,
yet he remained God. Do you want to have an
advocate in the Son's presence, too? Turn to Mary.

– St. Bernard of Clairvaux

Compassionate Mother, pray for us!

April 26

You [Mary] are a vessel containing every grace, the
fullness of all things good and beautiful, the tablet
and living icon of every good and all uprightness,
since you alone have been deemed worthy to receive
the fullness of every gift of the Spirit.

– St. Gregory Palamas

Sanctuary of the Holy Spirit, pray for us!

April 27

While remaining the mother of our Judge, Mary is a mother to us, full of mercy. She constitutes our protection. She keeps us close to Christ, and she faithfully takes the matter of our salvation into her charge.

– St. Peter Canisius

Mother of our Judge, pray for us!

April 28

As all perfection consists in our being conformed, united and consecrated to Jesus it naturally follows that the most perfect of all devotions is that which conforms, unites, and consecrates us most completely to Jesus. Now of all God's creatures Mary is the most conformed to Jesus. It therefore follows that, of all devotions, devotion to her makes for the most effective consecration and conformity to him. The more one is consecrated to Mary, the more one is consecrated to Jesus.

– St. Louis de Montfort

Mold of Holiness, pray for us!

April 29

Mary is the most sweet bait, chosen
by God, to catch men.

– ST. CATHERINE OF SIENA

Bait of God, pray for us!

April 30

Eternal Wisdom calls people's attention to
[Mary] her in order to use her as bait, as
magnet, as hook for human hearts.

– SERVANT OF GOD (FR.) JOSEPH KENTENICH

Conqueror of the Hearts of Men, pray for us!

INMACULATA VIRGINIS MARIÆ CONCEPTIO SIT NOBIS SALUS ET PROTECTIO

MAY

May 1

For her part, Mary is the living Church. It is upon her that the Holy Spirit descends, thereby making her the new Temple. Joseph, the just man, is appointed to be the steward of the mysteries of God, the *paterfamilias* and guardian of the sanctuary, which is Mary the bride and the Logos in her. He [Joseph] thus becomes the icon of the bishop, to whom the bride is betrothed; she is not at his disposal but under his protection.

– POPE BENEDICT XVI

Bride of St. Joseph, pray for us!

May 2

This blueprint love [The Blessed Virgin Mary], whom God loved before the world was made, this Dream Woman before women were, is the one of whom every heart can say in its depth of depths: "She is the woman I love!"

– VENERABLE FULTON J. SHEEN

Dream Woman, pray for us!

May 3

For as the dawn is the end of night, and the
beginning of day, well may the Blessed Virgin
Mary, who was the end of vices,
be called the dawn of day.

– POPE INNOCENT III

Dawn of Day, pray for us!

May 4

All of his divine attributes, in a manner of speaking,
attempted to outdo one another in order
to create a first-class masterpiece.

– SERVANT OF GOD (FR.) JOSEPH KENTENICH

Queen Conceived without Original Sin, pray for us!

May 5

Mary is the epitome of beauty. Masterpieces are never
partial beauties, but a synthesis of the beautiful:
Mary is the creature most clearly revealing
the divine Trinitarian presence.

– VENERABLE POPE PAUL VI

Masterpiece of Beauty, pray for us!

May 6

The Virgin Mary, among all creatures,
is a masterpiece of the Most Holy Trinity.

– POPE BENEDICT XVI

Masterpiece of the Holy Trinity, pray for us!

May 7

The most beautiful creature of all, the one in whom all the marvels and supernatural order are gathered, is Mary. She is God's masterpiece.

— BLESSED JAMES ALBERIONE

God's Masterpiece, pray for us!

May 8

Mary's vastness exceeds our capacity to exaggerate her. Our intelligence really cannot compass her. Necessarily God's masterpiece evades our full understanding so that when luminous glimpses are afforded to us we find the light too much.

— SERVANT OF GOD FRANK DUFF

Queen of Virgins, pray for us!

May 9

No one ever knew Christ so profoundly as she [Mary]
did, and no one can ever be a more competent guide
and teacher of the knowledge of Christ.

– St. Pope Pius X

Mother of the Word, pray for us!

May 10

If you could have preexisted your mother ... would you not
have made her the most perfect woman that ever lived —
one so beautiful she would have been the sweet envy of all
women, and one so gentle and so merciful that all other
mothers would have sought to imitate her virtues? Why,
then, should we think that God would do otherwise?

– Venerable Fulton J. Sheen

Queen Mother, pray for us!

May 11

O most loving Virgin, Mother of the Savior of all the
ages, from this day onward take me into your service.
And in every circumstance of my life, be with me
always, most merciful Advocatrix. Except for God,
I place nothing above you, and, as your own servant,
I freely place myself under your command forever.

– St. Odilo of Cluny

Advocatrix, pray for us!

May 12

No one is saved except through you, O All-Holy.
No one is delivered from evils except through you,
O All-Chaste. No one obtains the grace of mercy
except through you, O All-Honorable.

– St. Germanus of Constantinople

Mother of the Savior, pray for us!

May 13

It appears to be of tremendous importance to the living God, the One who rules and guides world history, that his Mother be glorified. By using instruments that are childlike and humble, courageous and trusting, he wants to have Mary's triumphal chariot drawn onto the battlefield of today's crisis-filled era, and in that way regain peace for the world. That is why God never tires of repeating, through the lips of the Popes, the last will and testament of our Savior — *ecce Mater tua.*

– SERVANT OF GOD (FR.) JOSEPH KENTENICH

Our Lady of Fatima, pray for us!

May 14

Four instincts deeply imbedded in the human heart: affection for the beautiful; admiration for purity; reverence for a Queen; and love of a Mother. All of these come to a focus in Mary.

– VENERABLE FULTON J. SHEEN

Mother Undefiled, pray for us!

May 15

O happy confidence! O perfect refuge! The Mother
of God is my Mother. What firm trust we should have,
then, since our salvation depends on the judgment
of a good brother and a tender Mother.

– St. Anselm of Canterbury

Mother of the Redeemer, pray for us!

May 16

Now if grace is beauty of spirit, what must be Mary's
beauty that surpasses all the beauty of the angels?

– St. Lawrence of Brindisi

Beauty of God, pray for us!

May 17

Let those who think that the Church pays too much
attention to Mary give heed to the fact that Our
Blessed Lord himself gave ten times as much of
his life to her as he gave to his apostles.

– VENERABLE FULTON J. SHEEN

Palace of the King, pray for us!

May 18

We have all that we have through Mary, and in her,
after God, we live and move and are.

– BLESSED STANISLAUS PAPCZYNSKI

Mystical Temple, pray for us!

May 19

Beauty is said to be a woman's honor. Physical beauty
is her honor among men; spiritual beauty is her
honor with God. How could anyone imagine that
God would deprive Mary of her honor?

– ST. LAWRENCE OF BRINDISI

Beautiful Lady, pray for us!

May 20

She [Mary] is the neck of Our Head,
by which he communicates to his
mystical body all spiritual gifts.

– ST. BERNARDINE OF SIENA

House of Gold, pray for us!

May 21

For women called to virginal chastity, Mary reveals
the lofty meaning of so special a vocation. Thus she
draws attention to the spiritual fruitfulness which
it produces in the divine plan: a higher order of
motherhood, a motherhood according to the Spirit.

– St. John Paul II

Glory of Virgins, pray for us!

May 22

If every woman were an image of the Mother of God,
a spouse of Christ and an apostle of the divine Heart,
she would fulfill her feminine vocation no matter in
what circumstances she lived and what her
external activities might be.

– St. Teresa Benedicta of the Cross

Apostle of the Divine Heart, pray for us!

May 23

Mary is the image and model of all mothers,
of their great mission to be guardians of life, of their
mission to be teachers of the art of living
and of the art of loving.

– POPE BENEDICT XVI

Guardian of Life, pray for us!

May 24

Take shelter under Our Lady's mantle, and do not
fear. She will give you all you need. She is
very rich, and besides is very generous
with her children. She loves giving.

– ST. RAPHAELA MARIA

Help of Christians, pray for us!

May 25

Heaven and earth praise her unceasingly, and are nevertheless unable to praise her as she deserves.

– St. Pope Gregory VII

Virgin Most Renowned, pray for us!

May 26

To begin and end well, devotion to our Blessed Lady, the Mother of God, is nothing less than indispensable.

– St. Philip Neri

Blessed Lady, pray for us!

May 27

A man is no true Christian if he has no devotion to the Mother of Jesus Christ.

– St. John Eudes

Our Lady of Ephesus, pray for us!

May 28

Let us run to Mary, and like little children, cast ourselves into her arms with perfect confidence.

– SAINT FRANCIS DE SALES

Anchor of Confidence, pray for us!

May 29

At the present moment it seems to be clearly in the plans of God, whose plans reveal themselves daily more and more, to glorify his Mother in a special manner, to show her to the nations as the Mediatrix of all Graces, and as the great Victress over the anthropological heresies.

– SERVANT OF GOD (FR.) JOSEPH KENTENICH

Victress of the Anthropological Heresies, pray for us!

May 30

Where Mary is, there is the archetype of total self-giving and Christian discipleship. Where Mary is, there is the Pentecostal breath of the Holy Spirit; there is new beginning and authentic renewal.

– POPE BENEDICT XVI

Spouse of the Holy Spirit, pray for us!

May 31

He hath regarded the humility of his handmaid; for behold from henceforth all generations shall call me blessed.

– LUKE 1:48

Mediatrix of All Grace, pray for us!

JUNE

June 1

The Church neglects one of the duties enjoined upon her when she does not praise Mary. She deviates from the word of the Bible when her Marian devotion falls silent. When this happens, in fact, the Church no longer even glorifies God as she ought.

– POPE BENEDICT XVI

Dwelling Place of the Holy Trinity, pray for us!

June 2

There never was, nor is, nor ever will be a grace given by God in any other way than by Mary's mediation.

– BLESSED MICHAEL SOPOCKO

Mother of Divine Grace, pray for us!

June 3

We must renew our devotion to the Blessed
Virgin if we wish to obtain the Holy Spirit and be
sincere followers of Christ Jesus.

– VENERABLE POPE PAUL VI

Our Lady of Akita, pray for us!

June 4

Mary becomes the "magnet" which attracts all
hearts to itself, the "lure" which attracts all like
fish and leads them into "God's net."

– SERVANT OF GOD (FR.) JOSEPH KENTENICH

Ravisher of Hearts, pray for us!

June 5

Mary is the mediatrix between us and Christ,
as Christ is between us and God. She is the
gate of heaven, for no one can enter
heaven unless it be through Mary.

– St. Bonaventure

Gate of Heaven, pray for us!

June 6

I trust you completely, Lord. Strengthen my
trust. In whom else can I hope, being so poor
and miserable in spirit, if not in your goodness,
if not in the heart of your Beloved Son, filled
with love and mercy; if not in the powerful
intercession of the most Blessed Virgin Mary?

– Blessed George Matulaitis

Virgin Most Prudent, pray for us!

June 7

Let us trust God through the Immaculate One with a limitless trust, and make every effort to the extent of our understanding and strength, to go forward, but in serenity of spirit, placing all our confidence in the Immaculate One.

– St. Maximilian Kolbe

Immaculate One, pray for us!

June 8

After God, we should have a great confidence in the Blessed Mother of Jesus, who is so good.

– St. John Vianney

Noble Maiden, pray for us!

June 9

She [Mary] alone is your [Jesus'] mother, but she is your sister, with everyone else. She was your mother, she was your sister, she was your bride, too, along with all chaste souls.

– St. Ephrem the Syrian

Bride of Christ, pray for us!

June 10

Let us fear and worship the undivided Trinity as we sing the praise of the ever-Virgin Mary, the holy temple of God, and of God himself, her Son and spotless Bridegroom.

– St. Cyril of Alexandria

Holy Temple of God, pray for us!

June 11

The flesh of Christ is the flesh of Mary, and although it was raised to great glory in his Resurrection, yet it still remained the same that was taken from Mary.

– St. Augustine of Hippo

Tabernacle of the Most High, pray for us!

June 12

Mary is the heart of the Church. This is why all works of charity spring from her. It is well known that the heart has two movements: systole and diastole. Thus Mary is always performing these two movements: absorbing grace from her Most Holy Son, and pouring it forth on sinners.

– St. Anthony Mary Claret

Heart of the Mystical Body, pray for us!

June 13

The Blessed Virgin did not lose the flower of her
virginity when she gave birth to the Savior.

– St. Anthony of Padua

Perpetual Virgin, pray for us!

June 14

The term "Woman" indicated a wider relationship to
all humanity than "Mother." It meant that she
[Mary] was to be not only his mother, but that she
was also to be the mother of all men, as he was the
Savior of all men. She was now to have many children
— not according to the flesh, but according to the
spirit. Jesus was her firstborn in the flesh in joy; John
was her second-born of the spirit in sorrow;
and we her millionth and millionth born.

– Venerable Fulton J. Sheen

Fruitful Mother, pray for us!

June 15

The Heart of Mary is the court where the
assizes of mercy are held.

– St. Madeleine Sophie Barat

Immaculate Heart of Mary, pray for us!

June 16

Mary is like the neck of the Mystical Body of the
Church, whose head is Christ, for in Christ we are all
one body. The neck is located above all the lower
members of the body and is immediately joined to
the head. The neck causes the head to bend.
Through Mary God bends down to us in mercy.

– St. Lawrence of Brindisi

Neck of the Mystical Body, pray for us!

June 17

Mary is not only the treasure, but the very
heart of the Church.

– St. John Eudes

Heart of the Church, pray for us!

June 18

Only through associating the Madonna with your
priesthood will you become efficacious in the
field of grace so as to make bud forth children
of God and saints in this world.

– St. Padre Pio

Queen of the Priesthood, pray for us!

June 19

The priest has a deep love of Mary not only in his better moments, but even in his failings. He trusts in her intercession to combat his weakness. Then especially, he looks to her for special attention, knowing that the child who falls most often is apt to get most of the mother's kisses.

– VENERABLE FULTON J. SHEEN

Protector of Priests, pray for us!

June 20

It is theologically and anthropologically important for women to be at the center of Christianity. Through Mary and the other holy women, the feminine element stands at the heart of the Christian religion.

– POPE BENEDICT XVI

Splendor of the Feminine Genius, pray for us!

June 21

Since Jesus is the Son of Mary's womb, we, too, are sons and daughters of that holy womb; her pure, virginal heart.

– SERVANT OF GOD MOTHER AUXILIA DE LA CRUZ

Fruitful Virgin, pray for us!

June 22

Since this blessed Lady Mary goes as a dawn between our night and the day of Christ, between our darkness and his brightness, and lastly between the misery of our sin and the mercy of God, to whom should wretched sinners turn for help, so as to be delivered quickly from their wretchedness and come to mercy, but to this Blessed Virgin Mary?

– ST. JOHN FISHER

Mary, the Dawn, pray for us!

June 23

In Paradise, Mary is as the Mother of a family. Give me an energetic mother, one well attentive to her house: she alone keeps an eye on everything; no matter how numerous the family is, she thinks of everything; she provides everyone with what is necessary; she does not even wait for one of the children to ask, she thinks of it; in fact, even before a thing becomes necessary, she prepares it so that it will be ready at the opportune moment. Isn't it true that a good mother does this? And this is precisely what Mary does. All of us form a large family of which God is the Head, the Father; the Mother of this great family, then, is Mary Most Holy. God has deposited all graces in her hands; and she, as a good mother, is always attentive to all our needs. She goes about distributing this grace to one and that to another, according to each one's particular needs: and at times she gives them to us without our asking for them.

– St. Joseph Cafasso

Mother of God's Family, pray for us!

June 24

The Eternal Father delights in regarding the Heart of the Blessed Virgin Mary as the masterpiece of his hands.

– ST. JOHN VIANNEY

Delight of the Father, pray for us!

June 25

She [Mary] is so beautiful that to see her again one would be willing to die.

– ST. BERNADETTE SOUBIROUS

Fountain of Beauty, pray for us!

June 26

Love of Our Lady is proof of a good spirit, in works and in individuals. Don't trust the undertaking that lacks this characteristic.

– ST. JOSEMARIA ESCRIVA

Mother of Good Counsel, pray for us!

June 27

We hail you, O Mary Mother of God, venerable treasure of the entire world, inextinguishable lamp, crown of virginity, scepter of orthodoxy, imperishable temple, container of him who cannot be contained, Mother and Virgin.

– St. Cyril of Alexandria

Scepter of Orthodoxy, pray for us!

June 28

The knot of Eve's disobedience was untied by Mary's obedience. What Eve bound through her unbelief, Mary loosed by her faith.

– St. Irenaeus of Lyons

Undoer of Knots, pray for us!

June 29

If Peter, from the fact that, by divine revelation, he professed Christ as the true Son of God and the Messiah, merited to be called blessed and to be made Christ's vicar, the rock of the Church and the keeper of the keys, what must we say of Mary?

– St. Lawrence of Brindisi

Queen of Apostles, pray for us!

June 30

Before the second coming of Christ, Mary, more than ever, must shine in mercy, might, and grace in order to bring unbelievers into the Catholic faith. The power of Mary in the latter days will be very conspicuous. Mary will extend the reign of Christ over the heathens and the Mohammedans, and it will be a time of great joy when Mary is enthroned as Mistress and Queen of Hearts.

– Venerable Mary of Agreda

Mistress and Queen of Hearts, pray for us!

JULY

July 1

The Blessed Virgin loves above all to see in her children
purity, humility, and charity.

– St. John Vianney

Lily of the Valley, pray for us!

July 2

She [Mary] is the woman every man marries in his ideal.

– Venerable Fulton J. Sheen

Heavenly Princess, pray for us!

July 3

O Mary, temple of the Trinity! O Mary, bearer of fire! Mary, minister of mercy! Mary, mother of the divine fruit! Mary, redemptress of the human race because it was by your flesh suffering in the Word that the world was redeemed!

– St. Catherine of Siena

Bearer of Fire, pray for us!

July 4

Mary [is] the pledge of divine mercy.

– St. Andrew of Crete

Pledge of Divine Mercy, pray for us!

July 5

In honoring Mary, in every thought of her,
we do homage to the superabundant mercy
and love of the Redeemer of men.

– VENERABLE POPE PIUS XII

Full of Mercy, pray for us!

July 6

In Mary we see how a truly good and provident
God has established for us a most suitable
example of every virtue.

– POPE LEO XIII

Model of Virtue, pray for us!

July 7

We cannot enter a house without first speaking to the porter. Similarly, we cannot enter heaven without calling upon the aid of the Blessed Virgin Mary who is the Portress of Heaven.

– ST. JOHN VIANNEY

Portress of Heaven, pray for us!

July 8

Looking at Mary, how can we, her children, fail to let the aspiration to beauty, goodness and purity of heart be aroused in us?

– POPE BENEDICT XVI

Rose Ever Blooming, pray for us!

July 9

She [Mary] participated in the same torments,
not by way of the executioners, like Jesus, but
she, by way of love and sorrow, participated in all
the torments, one by one. The heart of Jesus and
the heart of Mary both stood united in suffering
and in love, and this they offered to God
the Father for all of us mortals.

– St. Veronica Giuliani

Sorrowful Mother, pray for us!

July 10

Devotion to Mary has decisively contributed
to elevating the status of woman.

– Blessed James Alberione

Crown of Creation, pray for us!

July 11

Mary was a princess of God, and God gave
her the best blood of Israel.

– SERVANT OF GOD (FR.) PATRICK J. PEYTON

Daughter of Zion, pray for us!

July 12

Blessed are those who nourish a deep devotion to Mary.
Though she is mother of all, she harbors a special love for
those who turn to her with heartfelt devotion.

– ST. LAWRENCE OF BRINDISI

Majestic Queen, pray for us!

July 13

All through her life she [Mary] felt secure and
sheltered in the will and heart of God.

– SERVANT OF GOD (FR.) JOSEPH KENTENICH

Devoted Daughter of God, pray for us!

July 14

The more each one of us draws near to the
Immaculate, the more we will draw near to one
another: this unity is our strength.

– St. Maximilian Kolbe

Dwelling Place of the Most High, pray for us!

July 15

I have never read of any saint who did not have a
special devotion to the glorious Virgin.

– St. Bonaventure

Glorious Virgin, pray for us!

July 16

As a Marian vestment, the sacred
scapular is certainly a sign and guarantee of
the protection of the Mother of God.

– VENERABLE POPE PIUS XII

Our Lady of Mt. Carmel, pray for us!

July 17

The body of Christ that the most Blessed Virgin bore,
fostered in her bosom, wrapped in swaddling cloths, and
nurtured with maternal love, that body, I say, and without
doubt not any other, we now receive from the holy altar, and
we drink his blood as a sacrament of our redemption.

– ST. PETER DAMIAN

Altar of the Divinity, pray for us!

July 18

Women who in order to please men, fall prey to the infatuations of the times, deny their true essence and their mission for our present day. In order to overcome the Eve in our time, the bride of Christ must glowingly demonstrate by her being, by her every word and deed, that Mary is the protector of woman's nobility.

– SERVANT OF GOD (FR.) JOSEPH KENTENICH

Protector of Women's Nobility, pray for us!

July 19

Woman is made for the sacred. She is heaven's instrument on earth. Mary is the proto-type, the pattern-woman who fulfills in herself the deepest aspirations of the heart of every daughter of Eve.

– VENERABLE FULTON J. SHEEN

Daughter of Eve Unfallen, pray for us!

July 20

The nearer a thing approaches to its principle the more does it partake of the effect of that principle. But Christ is the principle of grace, and Mary is nearest to him, since he received from her his human nature. Hence she ought to receive from Christ a greater fullness of grace than anyone else.

– St. Thomas Aquinas

All-Chaste, pray for us!

July 21

My brothers, who but a total idiot could ever doubt that he would find water in the sea? So, too, when we come to Mary, can we have the least doubt that we will find grace and mercy in one who is the Mother of Grace, the Mother of Mercy, the Mother of Kindness, the sea of goodness, the ocean of love?

– St. Lawrence of Brindisi

Sea of Goodness, pray for us!

July 22

An infallible and unmistakable sign by which we can distinguish a heretic, a man of false doctrine, an enemy of God, from one of God's true friends is that the heretic and the hardened sinner show nothing but contempt and indifference for our Lady, and endeavor, by word and example, openly and insidiously — sometimes under specious pretexts — to belittle the love and veneration shown to her.

– St. Louis de Montfort

Queen Assumed into Heaven, pray for us!

July 23

There is no sinner in the world, however much at enmity with God, who cannot recover God's grace by recourse to Mary, and by asking her assistance.

– St. Bridget of Sweden

Tower of David, pray for us!

July 24

We are on the offensive, defending religion is too little for us; rather we are leaving the fortress and, confident in our Leader, going among the enemies and hunting for hearts in order to vanquish them for the Immaculate. ... Every heart which beats upon the earth and which shall beat, until the end of the world, must be prey for the Immaculate: this is our purpose.

– St. Maximilian Kolbe

Our Lady of Victory, pray for us!

July 25

By her intercession she [Mary] leads from heaven the army of apostles.

– Servant of God (Fr.) Joseph Kentenich

Marshal of the Armies of God, pray for us!

July 26

Imperial maiden and mistress, Queen, sovereign lady,
take me under thy protection, guard me lest Satan,
the author of destruction, rise up against me,
lest the accursed enemy triumph over me.

– St. Ephrem the Syrian

Daughter of Saints Joachim and Anne, pray for us!

July 27

Satan fears Mary as a frightened dog fears the rod
with which he has been beaten.

– St. John Eudes

Vanquisher of Satan, pray for us!

July 28

Providence ordinarily uses the initiative and activity of men to realize its designs. It follows that the Immaculate Virgin stood in need of soldiers ready to fight the battles of the Lord under her auspices. Providence must call forth such apostles; it must inspire them from on high; it must enroll them under her banner as her ministers and soldiers.

– BLESSED WILLIAM JOSEPH CHAMINADE

Battle Queen, pray for us!

July 29

Be her soldier so that others may become ever more perfectly hers, like you yourself, and even more than you; so that all those who live and will live all over the world may work together with her in her struggle against the infernal serpent.

– ST. MAXIMILIAN KOLBE

Imperial Maiden, pray for us!

July 30

He who is not awestruck by this Virgin's
spirit and who does not admire her soul is
ignorant of how great God is.

– St. Peter Chrysologus

Imperishable Temple, pray for us!

July 31

As the pseudo-reform of Luther and his accomplices
was met by an order justly renowned, assuming the
name and standard of Jesus, so too Providence will
now assign to its militia the name and standard of
Mary, enabling the knights of the new crusade to
hasten to and fro at the beck of their Queen, to
diffuse her devotion and, by the fact, to extend
the Kingdom of God in souls.

– Blessed William Joseph Chaminade

Queen of Knights, pray for us!

AUGUST

August 1

After the love which we owe Jesus Christ,
we must give the chief place in our heart
to the love of his Mother Mary.

– St. Alphonsus Liguori

Peaceful Dove, pray for us!

August 2

The priest has duties to fulfill toward this tender
Mother. He ought to be second to none in the honor
he renders her, the tender love that is due her. He
should most zealously make her known and loved.

– St. Peter Julian Eymard

Mother of Priests, pray for us!

August 3

With good reason does Sacred Scripture call Mary the "Valiant Woman," for she is the marshal of the armies of God himself and the principal enemy of the infernal serpent. The battalions of hell fear Mary far more than a small, weak body of foot soldiers would fear a powerful mechanized enemy force in battle array.

– St. John Eudes

Valiant Woman, pray for us!

August 4

The Blessed Virgin was the object of my earliest affections; I loved her even before I knew her.

– St. John Vianney

Promised Woman, pray for us!

August 5

My tongue preaches Mary; my favorite, most
frequent, and most ardent sermon will be the
Madonna. I will not miss an occasion to speak of
Mary and I will try my best to introduce this
subject whenever I can.

– BLESSED JAMES ALBERIONE

Our Lady of the Snows, pray for us!

August 6

Holy Virgin Mary, among all the women of the
world there is none like you. You are the
daughter and handmaid of the most high King
and Father of heaven.

– ST. FRANCIS OF ASSISI

Daughter of the Father, pray for us!

August 7

She [Mary] was formed in the heavens, and only
the Artificer who formed her is able to
comprehend her greatness.

– VENERABLE MARY OF AGREDA

Celestial Paradise, pray for us!

August 8

She [Mary] is the one whom every man loves when
he loves a woman — whether he knows it or not.

– VENERABLE FULTON J. SHEEN

Mystical Beauty, pray for us!

August 9

Every woman who wants to fulfill her destiny
must look to Mary as the ideal.

– St. Teresa Benedicta of the Cross

Princess of Heaven, pray for us!

August 10

This grand Princess [Mary] is the honor and
perfection of all in the order of nature, since in
her and by her the Creator of the world has
united himself to man.

– St. John Eudes

Grand Princess, pray for us!

August 11

Mary is the most loved and loving
Daughter of God the Father.

– BLESSED GABRIEL MARIA ALLEGRA

Daughter of God, pray for us!

August 12

My desire is for the young people of the entire world to
come closer to Mary. She is the bearer of an incredible
youthfulness and beauty that never wanes. May young
people have increasing confidence in her and may they
entrust the life just opening before them to her.

– ST. JOHN PAUL II

Bearer of Youthfulness and Beauty, pray for us!

August 13

Hail, thou fountain springing forth by God's
design, whose rivers flowing over in pure and
unsullied waves of orthodoxy put to
flight the hosts of error.

– St. Germanus of Constantinople

Our Lady of the Waves, pray for us!

August 14

We want her [Mary] to think, to speak and to
act through us. We desire to belong to the
Immaculate to the extent that nothing will
remain in us that is not her, so that we may be
annihilated in her, transubstantiated into her,
changed into her, that she alone remains, so that
we may be as much hers as she is God's.

– St. Maximilian Kolbe

Queen of Martyrs, pray for us!

August 15

In Mary God has given back woman's lost crown.
In her, woman has again become queen. The one
only purely created being who is allowed to enter
into the most intimate imaginable union with God is
a woman: the Queen of heaven and earth. In her,
all the members of her sex experience the solar
radiance of feminine dignity and beauty and
a piece of their own God-given greatness.

– SERVANT OF GOD (FR.) JOSEPH KENTENICH

Solar Radiance of Feminine Dignity, pray for us!

August 16

If we love our Mother, the Blessed Virgin, we
should make it both our duty and privilege to
have one of her pictures or statues in our home,
which from time to time will remind us of her.

– ST. JOHN VIANNEY

Queen of Families, pray for us!

August 17

In our day, Our Lady has been given to us as the
best defense against the evils that afflict modern
life; Marian devotion is the sure guarantee
of her maternal protection and safeguard
in the hour of temptation.

– POPE BENEDICT XVI

Mother of Perpetual Help, pray for us!

August 18

As no man goeth to the Father but by the Son,
so no man goeth to Christ but by his Mother.

– POPE LEO XIII

Woman of Cana, pray for us!

August 19

She is Heaven's masterpiece, the Empress of Heaven, its joy and its glory, in whom everything is heavenly.

– St. John Eudes

Empress of Heaven, pray for us!

August 20

De Maria Numquam Satis (Of Mary, Never Enough).

– St. Bernard of Clairvaux

Queen of All Hearts, pray for us!

August 21

God could have given us the Redeemer of the human race, and the Founder of our Faith, in another way than through the Virgin, but since Divine Providence has been pleased that we should have the Man-God through Mary, who conceived him by the Holy Ghost, and bore him in her womb, it remains for us to receive Christ only from the hands of Mary.

– St. Pope Pius X

Our Lady of Knock, pray for us!

August 22

Mary is a great Princess and a most powerful Queen; Queen of men and angels, Empress of the universe. She was Princess and Queen from the womb of her mother.

– St. John Eudes

Queen of all Creation, pray for us!

August 23

O wonderful girl, mother of her own creator! O stupendous honor, that a woman should have a son with God, to whom she may say, as the Father said: You are my Son (Ps 2:7), and that this girl should be the mother of one whose Father is God! The Son is seated at the right hand of the Father, the Mother at the right hand of the Son, and in turn they behold their common Son in their midst with happy gaze.

– St. Thomas of Villanova

Daughter of your Son, pray for us!

August 24

If Christ, the God-man, is the supreme and omnipotent Mediator by nature, Mary, the Mother of God, is Mediatrix by grace, as by grace she is omnipotent: her prayer is most efficacious and her mediation infallible.

– BLESSED LUIGI ORIONE

Mediatrix of Grace, pray for us!

August 25

The knight fights in dependence upon, by the wish and command, and for the honor of his Queen. In this case he fights for the spreading of her love and devotion with the stated intention so that the world, through you transformed, will pay due homage to your Son. This means the restoration of the world in Christ through Mary.

– SERVANT OF GOD (FR.) JOSEPH KENTENICH

Strength of Men, pray for us!

August 26

To serve Mary and to be her courtier is the greatest honor
one can possibly possess, for to serve the Queen of Heaven
is already to reign there, and to live under her
command is more than to govern.

– St. John Damascene

Our Lady of Czestochowa, pray for us!

August 27

The Immaculata must conquer the whole world for
herself, and each individual soul as well, so that she
can bring all back to God. This is why we must
acknowledge her for what she is, and submit to her
and to her reign, which is all gentleness.

–St. Maximilian Kolbe

Gentle Mother, pray for us!

August 28

Mary is the living mold of God.

– St. Augustine of Hippo

Living Mold of God, pray for us!

August 29

Saints are molded in Mary. There is a vast difference between carving a statue by blows of hammer and chisel and making a statue by using a mold. Sculptors and statue-makers work hard and need plenty of time to make statues by the first method. But the second method does not involve much work and takes very little time. St. Augustine speaking to our Blessed Lady says, "You are worthy to be called the mold of God." Mary is a mold capable of forming men into the image of the God-man. Anyone who is cast into this divine mold is quickly shaped and molded into Jesus and Jesus into him. At little cost and in a short time he will become Christ-like since he is cast into the very same mold that fashioned a God-man.

– St. Louis de Montfort

Mold of Eternal Wisdom, pray for us!

August 30

A tender devotion towards the Immaculate Mother
of God is one of the most powerful means of
counteracting within us the effects of the virus
emanating from the fatal tree of the terrestrial paradise.

– BLESSED ILDEFONSO SCHUSTER

Heavenly Nurse, pray for us!

August 31

Talking to Mary should be very simple. Many have
found the way easily. More should try it.

– SERVANT OF GOD CATHERINE DE HUECK DOHERTY

Mediatress, pray for us

SEPTEMBER

September 1

She [Mary] overcomes both the
Heart of God and the heart of man.

– Servant of God (Fr.) Joseph Kentenich

Dove of Beauty, pray for us!

September 2

The greatest saints were the most
ardent devotees of Mary.

– St. Vincent Pallotti

Standard of Holiness, pray for us!

September 3

Behold the power of the Virgin Mother: she wounded and took captive the heart of God.

– St. Bernardine of Siena

Sweetheart of God, pray for us!

September 4

I wish I could consecrate all souls to her, for it is she who leads us to Jesus: it is she that we must allow to live in us so that Christ can take the place of our nothingness: she is the safest, shortest, the most perfect way to lead us to the Infinite, to unite us with uncreated Love until we are lost in him, immersed in the Source of eternal bliss.

– Blessed Dina Belanger

Mystical Rose, pray for us!

September 5

Mary is our Co-redemptrix with Jesus. She gave Jesus his body and suffered with him at the foot of the Cross.

– Blessed Teresa of Calcutta

Co-redemptrix, pray for us!

September 6

There is no more excellent way to obtain graces from God than to seek them through Mary, because her divine Son cannot refuse her anything.

– St. Phillip Neri

Rose of Sharon, pray for us!

September 7

In the conception of Mary it was as if divine mercy and divine justice were running side by side. … Mercy outran justice and reached Mary sooner, because God by his very nature is much quicker at showing mercy than justice, especially when it concerns something in conformity with reason and common sense.

– St. Lawrence of Brindisi

Masterpiece of Mercy, pray for us!

September 8

Mary brings us the Bread of Life. From the day of her birth we salute her as the aurora of the Eucharist, for we know that the Savior of mankind will take from her the substance of that Body and Blood which he will give us in the Adorable Sacrament of his love.

– St. Peter Julian Eymard

Our Lady of the Most Blessed Sacrament, pray for us!

September 9

She is the standard of holiness, the model of virtue, the example of religion, the scourge of demons, the helper of men, and at last the summary, abridged and collected, of all brilliance and grace, in whom all the beauty and grace of angelic and human creation are ordered.

– St. Thomas of Villanova

Scourge of Demons, pray for us!

September 10

The name of the Mother of God contains all the history of the divine economy in this world.

– St. John Damascene

Mary, Mother of Christ, pray for us!

September 11

As wax melts before fire, so do the devils lose their
power against those souls who remember the
name of Mary and devoutly invoke it.

– ST. BONAVENTURE

Beloved Daughter of the Eternal Father, pray for us!

September 12

Men do not fear a powerful hostile army
as the powers of hell fear the name
and protection of Mary.

– ST. BONAVENTURE

Maria, pray for us!

September 13

Consecrating ourselves to Mary means accepting her help
to offer ourselves and the whole of mankind to him who
is holy, infinitely holy; it means accepting her help — by
having recourse to her motherly heart, which beneath the
cross was opened to love for every human being.

– St. John Paul II

Mystical Love, pray for us!

September 14

We will never be able to go deeply enough into
the stupendous fact of what God has
accomplished in Mary!

– Venerable Pope Paul VI

Paradise of God, pray for us!

September 15

A genuine child avoids everything that causes his mother sadness and sorrow. The greatest sorrow we can cause our Mother Thrice Admirable is sin, for it was sin that murdered her divine Son, that pierced her heart with a sevenfold sword. We show we are children of our Mother Thrice Admirable, therefore, when we foster a deep hatred of sin, and as soon as we are torn away by passion and fall into sin, to find our way to holy confession.

– SERVANT OF GOD (FR.) JOSEPH KENTENICH

Our Lady of Sorrows, pray for us!

September 16

When I sinned against the Son, I distressed the Mother; nor could I have offended the Mother without injuring the Son.

– ST. ANSELM OF CANTERBURY

Immaculate Victim, pray for us!

September 17

All favors, graces, and heavenly inspirations come
from Christ as from the Head. All then descend
to the body through Mary, since — just as
in the human body — it is by the neck
that the Head gives life to the limbs.

— ST. ROBERT BELLARMINE

New Eve, pray for us!

September 18

From the nature of his work the Redeemer ought to
have associated his Mother with his work. For this
reason we invoke her under the title of Co-redemptrix.
She gave us the Savior, she accompanied him in the
work of redemption as far as the Cross itself, sharing
with him the sorrows of the agony and of the death in
which Jesus consummated the redemption of mankind.

— POPE PIUS XI

Associate of the Redeemer, pray for us!

September 19

The sword that Christ ran into his own heart and
Mary's soul has become so blunted by the pressings
that it can never wound so fiercely again.

– VENERABLE FULTON J. SHEEN

Our Lady of LaSalette, pray for us!

September 20

I take refuge in Our Lady, with trust, with certitude
… I have carved her image so deeply in my heart that
no one will be able to take it away.

– VENERABLE BERNARD MARIA CLAUSI

Mary, Most Holy, pray for us!

September 21

Truly she has become the Lady ruler of every creature, since she is the Mother of the Creator.

– St. John Damascene

Mother of our Creator, pray for us!

September 22

Just as in the creation of the world, every creature was brought together in man (so he is called a microcosm, that is, a small world), so in the restoration of the world, the entire church and the perfection of saints were brought together in the Virgin; hence she may be called a microcosm of the church.

– St. Thomas of Villanova

Microcosm of the Church, pray for us!

September 23

Make every effort, like many elect souls, to follow
invariably this Blessed Mother, to walk close to
her since there is no other path leading to life
except the path followed by our Mother.

– ST. PADRE PIO

Path to Life, pray for us!

September 24

The heart of the divine Father belongs to Mary,
as the heart of the most loving of fathers to the
most devoted of daughters.

– ST. JOHN EUDES

Darling of God, pray for us!

September 25

Man beholds and experiences in Mary the shining
ideal of womanhood as it slumbers in his soul;
by it he develops into a personal, radiant totality
and produces an unaffected reverence toward
everyone who bears Mary's countenance.

– SERVANT OF GOD (FR.) JOSEPH KENTENICH

Shining Ideal of Womanhood, pray for us!

September 26

Mary, as the pattern both of maidenhood and
maternity, has exalted woman's state and nature,
and made the Christian virgin and the Christian
mother understand the sacredness of
their duties in the sight of God.

– BLESSED JOHN HENRY NEWMAN

Pattern of Maidenhood and Maternity, pray for us!

September 27

Glory of virgins, the joy of mothers, the support
of the faithful, the diadem of the Church,
the model of the true Faith, the seat of piety,
the dwelling place of the Holy Trinity.

– ST. PROCLUS OF CONSTANTINOPLE

Diadem of the Church, pray for us!

September 28

Whoever consistently looks at God and
themselves through this attractive mirror [Mary],
will sooner or later turn into another Mary.

– SERVANT OF GOD (FR.) JOSEPH KENTENICH

Mirror of Justice, pray for us!

September 29

God alone excepted, Mary is more excellent than all,
and by nature fair and beautiful, and more holy than
the Cherubim and Seraphim. To praise her all the
tongues of heaven and earth do not suffice.

– BLESSED POPE PIUS IX

Delight of the Angels, pray for us!

September 30

God is captivated by your grace and beauty [Mary]. As a
magnet draws iron, so your grace and beauty have drawn
God down from heaven to you. As Jacob was smitten with
love for Rachel, David for Bathsheba, Ahasuerus for Esther,
Adam for Eve, so God has fallen in love with you.

– ST. LAWRENCE OF BRINDISI

Bride of the Canticle, pray for us!

OCTOBER

October 1

Have no fear of loving the Blessed Virgin too much,
you will never love her enough, and Jesus will be
pleased since the Blessed Virgin is his Mother.

— St. Thérèse of Lisieux

Beauty of Virgins, pray for us!

October 2

If I call you the "beauty of God," you are worthy of
the name; if I call you "mistress of the angels,"
you are shown to be so in all things.

— St. Ambrose Autpert

Mistress of the Angels, pray for us!

October 3

The heart of a mother is a marvel of mercy. When we
fear to go to God, when we are overwhelmed by our
unworthiness, we can go to Mary, because God
has entrusted to her the realm of mercy.

– BLESSED COLUMBA MARMION

Marvel of Mercy, pray for us!

October 4

Hail, Lady, Holy Queen, Holy Mary, Mother of
God, who art virgin made church, and chosen
by the most Holy Father in heaven.

– ST. FRANCIS OF ASSISI

Virgin Made Church, pray for us!

October 5

O Mary, my Mother, and my Lady, I offer you
my soul, my body, my life and my death,
and all that will follow it. I place
everything in your hands.

– St. Faustina Kowalska

Mother of Divine Mercy, pray for us!

October 6

O Blessed Rosary of Mary, sweet chain which
binds us to God, bond of love which unites us to
the angels, tower of salvation against the assaults
of hell, safe port in our universal shipwreck,
we shall never abandon you.

– Blessed Bartolo Longo

Morning Star, pray for us!

October 7

I could conquer the world if I had
an army to say the Rosary.

— BLESSED POPE PIUS IX

Our Lady of the Rosary, pray for us!

October 8

Even if you have to fight distractions all through your
whole Rosary be sure to fight well, arms in hand: that
is to say, do not stop saying your Rosary even if it is
hard to say and you have absolutely no sensible
devotion. It is a terrible battle, I know, but one
that is profitable to the faithful soul.

— ST. LOUIS DE MONTFORT

Queen of the Most Holy Rosary, pray for us!

October 9

He [Jesus] became man of her; and received her lineaments
and her features as the appearance and character under
which he should manifest himself to the world. He was
known, doubtless, by this likeness to be her Son. Thus his
Mother is the first of the Prophets, for, of her, came the
Word bodily; she is the sole oracle of Truth, for the
Way, the Truth, and the Life vouchsafed to be her Son;
she is the one mold of Divine Wisdom,
and in that mold it was indelibly set.

– BLESSED JOHN HENRY NEWMAN

Mold of Divine Wisdom, pray for us!

October 10

It is mainly to expand the Kingdom of Christ that we
look to the Rosary for the most effective help.

– POPE LEO XIII

Victorious Lady, pray for us!

October 11

As an exercise of Christian devotion among the faithful of the Latin Rite who constitute a notable portion of the Catholic family, the Rosary ranks after Holy Mass and the Breviary for ecclesiastics [priests], and for the laity after participation in the sacraments. It is a devout form of union with God and lifts souls to a high supernatural plane.

– St. Pope John XXIII

Salus Populi Romani, pray for us!

October 12

Never will anyone really be able to understand the marvelous riches of sanctification which are contained in the prayers and mysteries of the Holy Rosary. This meditation on the mysteries of the life and death of Our Lord and Savior Jesus Christ is the source of the most wonderful fruits for those who use it.

– St. Louis de Montfort

Cause of our Joy, pray for us!

October 13

Day after day, our life and action is assimilated
anew to the *altera Maria*; and more and more,
in spite of all hindrances, we become an
apparition of Mary, at least in miniature.

– SERVANT OF GOD (FR.) JOSEPH KENTENICH

Woman Clothed with the Sun, pray for us!

October 14

The Rosary belongs among the finest
and most praiseworthy traditions of
Christian contemplation.

– ST. JOHN PAUL II

Woman of Prayer, pray for us!

October 15

If you wish to convert anyone to the fullness of the knowledge of our Lord and of his Mystical Body, then teach him the Rosary. One of two things will happen. Either he will stop saying the Rosary — or he will get the gift of faith.

– VENERABLE FULTON J. SHEEN

Woman of Faith, pray for us!

October 16

It is impossible to meditate with devotion upon the mysteries of the Rosary and live in a state of sin.

– ST. JOHN VIANNEY

Our Lady of Ransom, pray for us!

October 17

The Rosary is the most complete and easiest instruction about the Blessed Mother, and it is the source of devotion to the Divine Master.

— BLESSED TIMOTHY GIACCARDO

Model of Piety and Devotion, pray for us!

October 18

I beseech the Virgin Mary that she may keep you under the protection of her tender maternity.

— ST. FRANCIS DE SALES

Mother Most Chaste, pray for us!

October 19

No one knows the good Mother she has been to me.

— VENERABLE MATT TALBOT

Mother of Divine Providence, pray for us!

October 20

She existed in the Divine Mind as an Eternal Thought before there were any mothers. She is the Mother of mothers — she is the world's first love.

– VENERABLE FULTON J. SHEEN

World's First Love, pray for us!

October 21

O Most Pure, Most Holy and Immaculate Mary, above all, God made you beautiful, for he bestowed upon you the fullness of grace. I love you, I offer you my homage, and I desire to imitate you. By your Immaculate Conception please keep watch over me, and always accompany me until I die. Drive away from me Satan's temptations and snares. Obtain for me from your beloved Son the forgiveness of all my sins and temporal punishment. Supported by your love, may I be able to take delight together with you in full participation in the glory of eternal life.

– VENERABLE CASIMIR WYSZYNSKI

Queen of Angels, pray for us!

October 22

From Mary we learn to surrender to God's Will in all things. From Mary we learn to trust even when all hope seems gone.

– ST. JOHN PAUL II

Our Lady of the Pillar, pray for us!

October 23

We entrust ourselves to Mary because she dries our tears with compassion and with kindness comforts our hearts.

– ST. LUIGI GUANELLA

Compassionate Queen, pray for us!

October 24

Our Blessed Lady is my Mother, my Patroness, my Mistress, my Directress, and — after Jesus — my All!

– ST. ANTHONY MARY CLARET

Princess of God, pray for us!

October 25

Piety towards the most holy Virgin is the mark of a truly Catholic heart.

– ST. POPE JOHN XXIII

Queen of Prophets, pray for us!

October 26

Let us venerate Mary with every fiber of our being,
from the deepest part of our heart, because
this is the will of him who wanted us to
receive everything through Mary.

– St. Bernard of Clairvaux

Bridal Chamber of the Lord, pray for us!

October 27

The Church sees in Mary the highest expression
of the "feminine genius" and she finds in
her a source of constant inspiration.

– St. John Paul II

*Highest Expression of the
Feminine Genius, pray for us!*

October 28

She [Mary] is what every woman wants
to be when she looks at herself.

– Venerable Fulton J. Sheen

Bride of God, pray for us!

October 29

Accept me, O Mary, for thine own, and as thine, take
charge of my salvation. I will no longer be mine; to
thee do I give myself. If, during the time past I have
served thee ill, and lost so many occasions of
honoring thee, for the future I will be one of thy
most loving and faithful servants.

– St. Alphonsus Liguori

Cause of our Salvation, pray for us!

October 30

When we recall the virtues with which the Virgin Mary crushed the head of the dragon from hell, we fill all of hell with fear. By imitating and practicing these virtues, the faithful cannot stray from the path to salvation for they receive deliverance and help from their Lady.

– VENERABLE CASIMIR WYSZYNSKI

Our Lady of the Miraculous Medal, pray for us!

October 31

The serpent lifts up its head throughout the world, but at the same time the Immaculate One wipes him out with smashing victories.

– ST. MAXIMILIAN KOLBE

Terror of Demons, pray for us!

NOVEMBER

November 1

The greatest saints, those richest in grace and virtue,
will be the most assiduous in praying to the most
Blessed Virgin, looking up to her as the perfect model
to imitate and as a powerful helper to assist them.

– St. Louis de Montfort

Queen of All Saints, pray for us!

November 2

Oh, if all men but knew thy goodness! Certainly, they
would consecrate themselves entirely to thee. Thou
wouldst give them to thy Son, and thus every day
thousands of souls would be saved.

– St. John Eudes

Interceding Queen, pray for us!

November 3

Everything said about the *ecclesia* in the Bible is true of her [Mary], and vice versa: the Church learns concretely what she is and is meant to be by looking at Mary. Mary is her mirror, the pure measure of her being, because Mary is wholly within the measure of Christ and of God.

– POPE BENEDICT XVI

Blueprint of the Church, pray for us!

November 4

The hidden wish of every woman in history, the secret desire of every feminine heart, is fulfilled in that instant when Mary says: "*Fiat*" — "Be it done unto me according to thy word."

– VENERABLE FULTON J. SHEEN

Bride of the Holy Spirit, pray for us!

November 5

Your Creator has become your Spouse,
he has loved your beauty [Mary].

– ST. AMADEUS OF LAUSANNE

Chamber of Spiritual Nuptials, pray for us!

November 6

In the inspired Scriptures, what is said in a universal
sense of the virgin mother, the Church, is understood
in an individual sense of the Virgin Mary, and what is
said in a particular sense of the virgin mother Mary is
rightly understood in a general sense of the virgin
mother, the Church. When either is spoken of,
the meaning can be understood of both,
almost without qualification.

– BLESSED ISAAC OF STELLA

Pattern of the Church, pray for us!

November 7

The Church is not a manufactured item: she is, rather, the living seed of God that must be allowed to grow and ripen. This is why the Church needs the Marian mystery; this is why the Church herself is a Marian mystery.

– POPE BENEDICT XVI

Untarnished Image of the Church, pray for us!

November 8

If Christ is the most perfect Reconciler, he must have merited that someone be preserved from sin. Such a person is none other than his mother.

– BLESSED JOHN DUNS SCOTUS

Immaculate Dove, pray for us!

November 9

The Church is comparable to Mary; the Church is also virgin and mother, a fruitful virginity bringing forth the faithful members of Christ's Mystical Body.

– St. Augustine of Hippo

Exemplar of the Church, pray for us!

November 10

For every man who is born again, the water of baptism is like the virginal womb. The same Spirit that filled the Virgin now fills the baptismal font.

– St. Leo the Great

Fountain of Salvation, pray for us!

November 11

May she throw about the Church today, as in times
gone by, the mantle of her protection and obtain
from God that now at least the Church and all
mankind may enjoy more peaceful days.

– VENERABLE POPE PIUS XII

Queen of Peace, pray for us!

November 12

We call the Church by the name of
Mary, for she deserves a double name.

– ST. EPHREM THE SYRIAN

Icon of the Church, pray for us!

November 13

Your name, O Mary, is a precious ointment,
which breathes forth the odor of Divine grace.
Let this ointment of salvation enter the
inmost recesses of our souls.

– St. Ambrose

Our Lady of Beauraing, pray for us!

November 14

She [Mary] is the cause of what came before her, the
champion of what came after her and the agent of
things eternal. She is the substance of the prophets,
the principles of the apostles, the firm foundation of
the martyrs and the premise of the teachers of the
Church. She is the glory of those upon earth, the joy
of celestial beings, the adornment of all creation. She
is the beginning and the source and the root of
unutterable good things; she is the summit and
the consummation of everything holy.

– St. Gregory Palamas

Joy of Celestial Beings, pray for us!

November 15

The axis of mercy supporting the world turns on
these hinges or poles, that through the Mother
we have access to the Son and through the Son to
the Father, so that being thus led we should have
no fear that our reconciliation would be rejected.

– ST. ALBERT THE GREAT

Shrine of Divine Mercy, pray for us!

November 16

Only by being another "Mary" for Jesus will they
[souls] be capable of being transformed.

– SERVANT OF GOD MOTHER AUXILIA DE LA CRUZ

Model of Saints, pray for us!

November 17

It would be more advantageous for the world to be without the sun, moon, and stars than to be without Mary. Mary is of greater benefit to the world than the sun and moon and stars of the firmament.

– St. Lawrence of Brindisi

Empress of the Universe, pray for us!

November 18

When the ship of the Church casts anchor at both moorings, not only at Christ's, but also at Mary's, it will sail successfully through all storms.

– Servant of God (Fr.) Joseph Kentenich

Unsinkable Ark, pray for us!

November 19

She [Mary] is the ark of Noah, in which the future generation of the world was preserved.

– St. Thomas of Villanova

Spiritual Vessel, pray for us!

November 20

O man, run through all creation with your thought, and see if there exists anything comparable to or greater than the holy Virgin, Mother of God. Circle the whole world, explore all the oceans, survey the air, question the skies, consider all the unseen powers, and see if there exists any other similar wonder in the whole creation.

– St. Proclus of Constantinople

Glory of Creation, pray for us!

November 21

There has never been a woman, even the most
beautiful, gracious, and lovely, who has had such
power over her most passionate and loving
husband, as Mary did over God because
of her grace and beauty.

— St. Lawrence of Brindisi

Spotless Dove of Beauty, pray for us!

November 22

Unless one looks to the Mother of God,
it is impossible to understand the
mystery of the Church.

— St. John Paul II

Splendor of the Church, pray for us!

November 23

The Church must relearn her
ecclesial being from Mary.

– POPE BENEDICT XVI

Treasure House of God's Mercy, pray for us!

November 24

At the time of the deluge even brutes were saved in
Noah's Ark. Under the mantle of Mary even sinners
obtain salvation. … Let us, then enter this ark, let us
take refuge under the mantle of Mary, and she most
certainly will not reject us, but will secure our salvation.

– ST. ALPHONSUS LIGOURI

Mother Uncorrupt, pray for us!

November 25

God could create an infinity of suns, one more
brilliant than the other, an infinity of worlds, one
more marvelous that the other, an infinity of angels,
one more holy than the other. But a creature more
holy, more ravishing, more gracious than his mother
he could not make; for in making her his Mother, he
gave her at once, so to say, all that he could give of
beauty and goodness and holiness and sanctity
in the treasury of his omnipotence.

– ST. LEONARD OF PORT MAURICE

Heaven's Masterpiece, pray for us!

November 26

A devotee of Mary will be saved;
a great devotee of Mary will become a saint.

– BLESSED JAMES ALBERIONE

Saint-Maker, pray for us!

November 27

She [Mary] is the key to paradise. In her let us place
all our hope, because we can expect all things
from God through her mediation.

– ST. FRANCIS ANTHONY FASANI

Ark of the Covenant, pray for us!

November 28

Mary is like that single opening in Noah's ark, through
which the remaining few of the human race and their
offspring were preserved from the great flood.

– ST. LAWRENCE OF BRINDISI

Our Lady of Kibeho, pray for us!

November 29

Mary constitutes for the Church
her truest image.

– POPE BENEDICT XVI

Image of the Church, pray for us!

November 30

Mary is our advocate, the mother of grace and mercy.
She is not ungrateful to those who serve her; she
never forgets and always rewards them. She is like a
fiery chariot because she conceived within her the
Word, the only-begotten Son of God. She carries and
spreads the fire of love because her Son is love.

ST. CATHERINE OF SIENA

Advocate of Eve, pray for us!

DECEMBER

December 1

In the Church's liturgy, Advent is a Marian season.
It is the season in which Mary made room in her womb
for the world's Redeemer and bore the expectation and
hope of humanity. To celebrate Advent means: to
become Marian, to enter into that communion
with Mary's Yes which, ever anew, is room for
God's birth, for the "fullness of time."

– POPE BENEDICT XVI

God-Bearer, pray for us!

December 2

He [Jesus] was Blessed Mary's food, her Son, the
honey of angels, the sweetness of all the saints. Her
life was sustained by him whom she fed. The Son,
to whom she gave milk to drink, gave her life.

– ST. ANTHONY OF PADUA

Mother of the Eucharist, pray for us!

December 3

The Immaculata alone has from God the promise of victory over Satan. She seeks souls that will consecrate themselves entirely to her, that will become in her hands forceful instruments for the defeat of Satan and the spread of God's kingdom.

– ST. MAXIMILIAN KOLBE

Prize of Warriors, pray for us!

December 4

What is sweeter than the Mother of my God? She has taken my mind captive; she has taken possession of my tongue; she is on my mind day and night.

– ST. JOHN DAMASCENE

Holy Queen, pray for us!

December 5

Nothing is too much when it comes to
honoring the Immaculate Virgin.

– St. Faustina Kowalska

Purest of All Lilies, pray for us!

December 6

In the Immaculate Conception, the Eternal Father
prepared her to be the Mother of Mercy by
preserving her from original sin and filling her with
sanctifying grace and the infused virtues, which he
poured out on her as on no other human creature.

– Blessed Michael Sopocko

Immaculate Virgin, pray for us!

December 7

I thank you, Lord, for having given me such extraordinary feelings of love for the Immaculate Conception of the Blessed Virgin Mary.

– BLESSED GEORGE MATULAITIS

Mary Immaculate, pray for us!

December 8

Immaculata Virginis Mariae Conceptio, sit nobis salus et protectio (May the Virgin Mary's Immaculate Conception, be our health and our protection).

– BLESSED STANISLAUS PAPCZYNSKI

Immaculate Conception, pray for us!

December 9

The Immaculate must be the Queen over all nations,
and this as soon as possible, and not only over all
taken together as a whole, but over each person
individually. Whoever goes contrary to this and
refuses to believe in her love, will perish.

– ST. MAXIMILIAN KOLBE

Immaculate Queen, pray for us!

December 10

The Immaculate Conception of the Virgin is a pledge
of salvation for every human creature.

– ST. JOHN PAUL II

Pledge of Salvation, pray for us!

December 11

The Immaculate Conception is the promising
dawn of the radiant day of Christ.

– ST. JOHN PAUL II

Our Lady of the Dawn Gate, pray for us!

December 12

Am I not here, I who am your Mother?
Are you not under my shadow and protection?
Am I not the source of your joy?
Are you not in the hollow of my mantle, in the
crossing of my arms? Do you need anything more?
Let nothing else worry you, or disturb you.

– OUR LADY'S WORDS TO ST. JUAN DIEGO

Our Lady of Guadalupe, pray for us!

December 13

Maintain an earnest admiration for the Immaculate.
Never be afraid that you might exalt her too much,
she who will shine throughout eternity as God's
masterpiece, as the most wonderful of his creatures,
as the brightest mirror of the divine perfections.

—VENERABLE POPE PIUS XII

Mirror of the Divine Perfections, pray for us!

December 14

Among creatures no one knows Christ better than
Mary; no one can introduce us to a profound
knowledge of his mystery better than his Mother.

— ST. JOHN PAUL II

Holy Virgin of Virgins, pray for us!

December 15

If the Church gives birth to the members of Christ,
then the Church greatly resembles Mary.

— St. Augustine of Hippo

Sanctuary of God, pray for us!

December 16

If the Church shows respect and veneration for everything
that came in contact with the Savior's Body, the cross, the
nails, the thorns, the winding sheet of his sepulcher, the
swathing bands of his infancy and similar things, what honor
must be due to this venerable body of the Blessed Virgin
from which the Body of the Redeemer was formed!

— St. John Eudes

Venerable Maiden, pray for us!

December 17

Many not understanding you, Mary, don't know how
to love you. They think there should be no one
between them and God. They don't realize that your
sole interest lies in bringing us closer to God.

– SERVANT OF GOD (FR.) PATRICK J. PEYTON

Mediatrix of God, pray for us!

December 18

She is the sanctuary, she is the mercy seat, she is the
ark of the covenant, she is the urn containing the
endlessly sweet manna from heaven.

– ST. THOMAS OF VILLANOVA

Mercy Seat, pray for us!

December 19

Consider this great mystery! The Son of God has passed whole and entire, from the heart of the Father to the womb of Mary, and from the womb of the Mother to the lap of the Church.

– ST. PETER DAMIAN

Treasure of the Church, pray for us!

December 20

There is no danger of exaggerating. We can never hope to fathom this inexpressible mystery [Mary's divine maternity] nor will we ever be able to give sufficient thanks to our Mother [Mary] for bringing us into such intimacy with the Blessed Trinity.

– ST. JOSEMARIA ESCRIVA

Adorer of the Trinity, pray for us!

December 21

In a certain sense Mary lived her Eucharistic faith
before the institution of the Eucharist, by the very
fact that she offered her virginal womb
for the Incarnation of God's Word.

– ST. JOHN PAUL II

Eucharistic Woman, pray for us!

December 22

O womb, in which the decree of our liberation was
composed! O belly, in which were forged
weapons to oppose the devil!

– ST. PROCLUS OF CONSTANTINOPLE

Birthplace of God, pray for us!

December 23

If God labored six days in preparing a paradise for man, he would spend a longer time preparing a paradise for his Divine Son. As no weeds grew in Eden, so no sin would arise in Mary, the paradise of the Incarnation. Most unbecoming it would be for the sinless Lord to come into the world through a woman afflicted with sin. A barn door cannot fittingly serve as an entrance to a castle.

– Venerable Fulton J. Sheen

God's Eden, pray for us!

December 24

Hapless are they who neglect Mary under pretext of the honor be paid to Jesus Christ! As if the Child could be found elsewhere than with the Mother!

– St. Pope Pius X

Celestial Princess, pray for us!

December 25

While we adore the Child, should we not then venerate his mother, and while we kneel to Jesus, should we not at least clasp the hand of Mary for giving us such a Savior? There is a grave danger that, lest in celebrating a Christmas without the mother, we may soon reach a point where we will celebrate Christmas without the Babe, and these days are upon us now.

– VENERABLE FULTON J. SHEEN

Theotokos, pray for us!

December 26

The Infant Jesus doesn't preach, or perform any miracles; he just receives the sweet caresses of his dearest mother because that is the will of his Father, who is in heaven.

– SERVANT OF GOD MOTHER AUXILIA DE LA CRUZ

Mother of Fairest Love, pray for us!

December 27

By asking the beloved disciple to treat Mary
as his mother, Jesus founded Marian devotion.

– St. John Paul II

Beautiful Mother, pray for us!

December 28

If Mary could make God small, she could also make
him big and, indeed, she did. For Mary conceived
him and carried him in her womb, and gave him
birth, and nursed him, and raised him.
What a marvelous work!

– St. Lawrence of Brindisi

Architect of the God-man, pray for us!

December 29

The Eucharist began at Bethlehem in Mary's arms. It was she who brought to humanity the Bread for which it was famishing, and which alone can nourish it. She it was who took care of that Bread for us. It was she who nourished the Lamb whose life-giving Flesh we feed upon. She nourished him with her virginal milk; she nourished him for the sacrifice, for she foreknew his destiny.

— ST. PETER JULIAN EYMARD

Mother of our Eucharistic Bread, pray for us!

December 30

Jesus, in the manger you didn't take the gifts for yourself that were offered. You left them all for Mary, your mother.

— SERVANT OF GOD MOTHER AUXILIA DE LA CRUZ

Princess of Bethlehem, pray for us!

December 31

She [Mary] holds all the great Truths of Christianity together, as a piece of wood holds a kite. Children wrap the string of a kite around a stick and release the string as the kite climbs to the heavens. Mary is like that piece of wood. Around her we wrap all the precious strings of the great Truths of our holy Faith — for example, the Incarnation, the Eucharist, the Church. No matter how far we get above the earth, as the kite may, we always have need of Mary to hold the doctrines of the Creed together. If we threw away the stick, we would no longer have the kite; if we threw away Mary, we would never have Our Lord. He would be lost in the Heavens, like our runaway kite, and that would be terrible, indeed, for us on earth.

— VENERABLE FULTON J. SHEEN

Pearl of Virgins, pray for us!

REFERENCES

AAS   *Acta Apostolicae Sedis* (Vatican City, 1909-)
PL   *Patrologia Latina*. J.P. Migne (ed.) 221 vols. (Paris, 1841-1864)
PG   *Patrologia Graeca*. J.P. Migne (ed.) 161 vols. (Paris, 1857-1866)

Introduction: Pope Francis, *Angelus Message* (September 8, 2013)

January 1: St. Albert the Great, as quoted in Luigi Gambero, S.M., *Mary in the Middle Ages: The Blessed Virgin Mary in the Thought of Medieval Latin Theologians*. Trans. Thomas Buffer (San Francisco: Ignatius Press, 2005), 226.

January 2: St. Louis de Montfort, *True Devotion to the Blessed Virgin* (Bay Shore, NY: Montfort Publications, 1980), 12. Used with permission.

January 3: Ven. Fulton J. Sheen, *Three to Get Married*. (Princeton, NJ: Scepter Publishers, 1951), 162.

January 4: Bl. Geurric of Igny, PL 185, 188.

January 5: Bl. William Joseph Chaminade, "Society of Mary Considered as a Religious Order," in *Spirit of Our Foundation: Volume I* (Dayton, OH: St. Mary's Convent, 1911), 144.

January 6: Servant of God (Fr.) Joseph Kentenich, *Called, Consecrated, Sent: Selected Texts of Father Joseph Kententich about the Priesthood*. (ed.) Peter Wolf (Waukesha, WI: Schoenstatt Editions USA, 2009), 116. Original German text, Berufen-geweiht-gesandt, copyright 2009, Schönstatt-Verlag, Vallendar. Used with permission.

January 7: Ven. Fulton J. Sheen, *Three to Get Married*, 168.

January 8: St. John Eudes, *The Admirable Heart of Mary*. Trans. Charles di Targiani & Ruth Hauser (Buffalo, NY: Immaculate Heart Publications, 1947), 126.

January 9: St. Peter Damian, PL 144, 743C.

January 10: St. Maximilian Kolbe, (*Scritti* 1295, III: 696), as quoted in James McCurry, O.F.M., Conv., "The Mariology of Maximilian Kolbe," *Marian Studies: Volume 36* (1985): 96.

January 11: Pope Leo XIII, *Augustissimae Virginis Mariae*, 9.

January 12: Bl. Marguerite Bourgeoys, as quoted in Ronda De Sola Chervin, *Quotable Saints* (Oak Lawn, IL: CMJ Marian Publishers, 1992), 95.

January 13: St. Hilary of Poitiers, as quoted in Pope Benedict XVI, *"Message for the Sixteenth World Day of the Sick"* (January 11, 2008).

January 14: St. Ildephonsus of Toledo, PL 96, 58 A – 59 B.

January 15: Servant of God Mother Auxilia de la Cruz, *The Eucharistic Life*. Trans. Maria Victoria Hernandez, O.P. (Washington, DC: Oblate Sisters, 2001), 69.

January 16: Servant of God Archbishop Luis M. Martinez, *Only Jesus.* Trans. Sr. Mary St. Daniel, B.V.M. (St. Louis, MO: B. Herder Book Co., 1962), 175.

January 17: St. Fulgentius, as quoted in Francis Edward Nugent, *Fairest Star Of All: A Little Treasury of Mariology* (Patterson, NJ: St. Anthony Guild Press, 1956), 25. Used with permission.

January 18: St. Maximilian Kolbe, *Maria Was His Middle Name*. Trans. Regis N. Barwig. (Altadena, CA: Benziger Sisters Publishers, 1977), 96-97.

January 19: Pope Benedict XVI, *"Message for the Sixteenth World Day of the Sick,"* (January 11, 2008).

January 20: St. John Paul II, as quoted in Arthur Burton Calkins, *Totus Tuus: John Paul II's Program of Marian Consecration and Entrustment* (New Bedford, MA: Academy of the Immaculate, 1992), 266.

January 21: St. Vincent Pallotti, as quoted in *Sayings of a Saint: Selections from the Writings of St. Vincent Pallotti.* (ed.) Augustine Kolencherry, S.A.C. (Bangalore, India: Asian Trading Corporation, 1989), 116.

January 22: Bl. William Joseph Chaminade, *"Aux Predicateurs de Retraites,"* (24 août 1839), Lettres de M Chaminade, Tome V, pp. 69-80 (No 1163) English translation: W. Joseph Chaminade, Letter to the Retreatmasters of 1839, or Circular on the Vow of Stability, trans. Carl Dreisoerner, S.M., (Kirkwood, Missouri: Maryhurst Press, 1937).

January 23: St. Ildelphonsus of Toledo, PL 96, 105 B – 106 B.

January 24: St. Francis de Sales, *The Sermons of St. Francis de Sales on Our Lady* (Rockford, IL: Tan Books, 1985), 148.

January 25: Bl. Guerric of Igny, as quoted in Rev. Charles G. Fehrenbach, C.SS.R (ed.) *Mary, Day By Day: Marian Meditations for Every Day taken from the Holy Bible and the Writings of the Saints* (New York: Catholic Book Publishing Corp., 1987), 156. Used with permission.

REFERENCES

January 26: St. Pope Pius X, in Nugent, 1.

January 27: Bl. George Matulaitis, as quoted in *Marian Prayers* (Rome-Stockbridge: Congregation of Marian Fathers, 2010), 6. Used with permission.

January 28: St. Thomas Aquinas, *In Salutationem Angelica* (On the Angelic Salutation). Trans. from the Latin text of the Marietti Edition, 1954, no. 13.

January 29: St. Ephrem the Syrian, as quoted in Ronald N. Beshara, *Mary: Ship of Treasures* (Lebanon: Diocese of Saint Maron – USA, 1988), 35.

January 30: St. John Eudes, *The Wondrous Childhood of the Most Holy Mother of God* (Albany, NY: Preserving Christian Publications, Inc., 2000), 42.

January 31: St. John Bosco, as quoted in Pamela Moran (ed.), *A Marian Prayer Book: A Treasury of Prayers, Hymns, and Meditations* (Ann Arbor, MI: Servant Publications, 1991), 57.

February 1: St. Bernard of Clairvaux, in Kentenich, *Mary, Our Mother and Educator: An Applied Mariology*, 64.

February 2: St. Louis de Montfort, *True Devotion*, 17. Used with permission.

February 3: Vatican Council II (*Lumen Gentium*, Chapter 8).

February 4: Servant of God (Fr.) Joseph Kentenich, *Mary, Our Mother and Educator: An Applied Mariology*. Trans. Jonathan Niehaus (Waukesha, WI: Schoenstatt Sisters of Mary, 1987), 71. Original text in German: Copyright 1973, under the title *Maria-Mutter und Erzieherin. Eine angewandte Mariologie*, Schönstatt-Verlag, Vallendar, Schönstatt, West Germany. Used with permission.

February 5: Pope Benedict XVI (Joseph Cardinal Ratzinger) & Vittorio Messori. *The Ratzinger Report: An Exclusive Interview on the State of the Church.* Trans. Salvator Attanasio & Graham Harrison. (San Francisco: Ignatius Press, 1985), 105.

February 6: St. Bernard of Clairvaux, as quoted in Msgr. Joseph Clifford Fenton "Our Lady and the Extirpation of Heresy," in *Studies in Praise of our Blessed Mother: Selections from the American Ecclesiastical Review.* (ed.) Msgr. Joseph C. Fenton & Edmond D. Benard (Washington, DC: Catholic University of America Press, 1952), 232.

February 7: Bl. Pope Pius IX, *Ineffabilis Deus*, 22-23.

February 8: Servant of God (Fr.) Joseph Kentenich, *Marian Instrument Piety* (Waukesha, WI: International Schoenstatt Center, 1992), 115. Complete German edition – Marianische Werkzeugsfrömmigkeit, written in Dachau, 1944, copyright 1974, Schönstatt-Verlag, Vallendar-Schönstatt, Germany. Used with permission.

February 9: Bl. Anne Catherine Emmerich, *The Life of the Blessed Virgin Mary*. Trans. Sir Michael Palairet (London: Burns & Oates, 1954), 145.

February 10: Servant of God Mother Auxilia de la Cruz, The Eucharistic Life, 67.

February 11: Bl. William Joseph Chaminade, *Letters of Father Chaminade*, Vols. 1-8. (Dayton, OH: Marianist Resources Commission, 1976-1986), no. 188.

February 12: St. Faustina Kowalska, *Diary: Divine Mercy in My Soul*. (Stockbridge, MA: Marian Press, 2002), no. 1746. Used with permission.

February 13: Servant of God (Fr.) Joseph Kentenich, Marian Instrument Piety, 116. Used with permission.

February 14: St. Methodius of Philippi, Oration on Simeon and Anna, as quoted in Jimmy Akin, *The Fathers Know Best: Your Essential Guide to the Teachings of the Early Church* (San Diego, CA: Catholic Answers, 2010), 345-346.

February 15: Bl. Michael Sopocko, *The Mercy of God In His Works: Volume IV*. Trans. R. Batchelor. (Hereford: Marian Apostolate, 1972), 83.

February 16: Bl. Guerric of Igny, as quoted in Deyanira Flores, "Forming Her Only-Begotten In The Sons By Adoption: The Marian Spirituality of Bl. Guerric of Igny (1157)," *Marian Studies,* Vol. LII (2001), 106.

February 17: St. Alphonsus Ligouri, *The Glories of Mary* (Rockford, IL: Tan, 1977), 136.

February 18: St. Vincent Pallotti, in Fehrenbach, *Mary, Day By Day, 17.*

February 19: Ven. Fulton J. Sheen, *The World's First Love: Mary, Mother of God* (San Francisco: Ignatius Press, 1996), 260. Used with permission.

February 20: St. Louis de Montfort, *True Devotion*, 9. Used with permission.

February 21: St. Peter Damian, PL 144, 743B.

February 22: Pope Leo XIII, *Adiutricem*, 17.

February 23: St. Bernardine of Siena, as quoted in Paul Haffner, *The Mystery of Mary* (England: Gracewing, 2004), 259.

February 24: Pope Benedict XVI, "Meeting with clergy of the Dioceses of Belluno-Feltre and Treviso," (July 24, 2007).

February 25: St. John Vianney, in Nugent, 26. Used with permission.

February 26: Ven. Teresa of Jesus Quevedo, as quoted in Ann Ball, *Modern Saints: Their Lives and Faces* (Rockford, IL: Tan Books, 1983), 396.

February 27: St. Gabriel Possenti, in Ball, 33.

February 28: St. Bernard of Clairvaux, PL 183, 100.

REFERENCES

February 29: Pope Francis, May 4, 2013, Papal address during recital of the Rosary at the Basilica of St. Mary Major in Rome, as quoted in "Under the Sign of the Protoevangelium," by Fr. Peter Damian M. Fehlner, F.I., in *Missio Immaculatae* Vol. 9/No.4 July/August 2013: 13.

March 1: St. Germanus of Constantinople, PG 98, 379-380.

March 2: Bl. Henry Suso, in Kentenich, *Mary, Our Mother and Educator: An Applied Mariology*, 144. Used with permission.

March 3: St. Alphonsus Ligouri, *The Glories of Mary*, 125-126.

March 4: Bl. James Alberione, *Mary, Hope of the World*. Trans. Hilda Calabro (Boston, MA: Daughters of St. Paul, 1981), 36.

March 5: St. Louis de Montfort, *True Devotion*, 88. Used with permission.

March 6: St. Bernard of Clairvaux, in Fehrenbach, *Mary, Day By Day*, 63.

March 7: St. Lawrence of Brindisi, *Mariale: Opera Omnia [Collected Sermons and Homilies of St. Lawrence of Brindisi]*. Trans. Vernon Wagner, O.F.M., Cap. (Delhi, India: Media House, 2007), 370.

March 8: Bl. William Joseph Chaminade, as quoted in *From A Full Heart: Thoughts from Father Chaminade* (North American Center for Marianist Studies, NACMS). Compiled by Francis J. Greiner, S.M., (St. Meinard, IN: The Grail Press, 1949), entry for September 8.

March 9: St. John Paul II, *Redemptoris Mater*, 21.

March 10: St. Bonaventure, in Gambero, *Mary in the Middle Ages*, 211.

March 11: St. John Paul II, (General Audience, May 11, 1983).

March 12: St. Peter Damian, PL 144, 740 C.

March 13: St. Albert the Great, in Gambero, *Mary in the Middle Ages*, 229.

March 14: Pope Benedict XVI, (Homily at Mass for the canonization of St. Anthony of St. Anne Galvao, Aparecida, Brazil, May 11, 2007).

March 15: St. John Vianney, as quoted in Jill Haak Adels, *The Wisdom of the Saints: An Anthology* (New York: Oxford University Press, 1987), 19.

March 16: St. Therese of Lisieux, as quoted in Francis W. Johnston (ed.) *The Voice of the Saints: Counsels from the Saints to bring comfort and guidance in daily living* (Rockford, IL: Tan Books, 1986), 142.

March 17: Bl. Michael Sopocko, *The Mercy of God*, 90.

March 18: St. Anselm of Lucca, as quoted in "Discovering Mary in the Middle Ages:

St. Anselm of Lucca (1086); Mary's Maternal Intercession," by Deyanira Flores, STD in *Queen of All Hearts*, May-June 1996, 26.

March 19: Bl. William Joseph Chaminade, *From A Full Heart*, entry for March 12.

March 20: Bl. Michael Sopocko, *God is Mercy: Meditations on God's most consoling attribute*. (Stockbridge, MA: Marian Fathers, 1965), 53. Used with permission.

March 21: St. John Eudes, *The Admirable Heart of Mary*, 290.

March 22: St. Bernardine of Siena, in Adels, 18.

March 23: St. Peter Faber, in Kentenich, *Mary, Our Mother and Educator: An Applied Mariology*, 66. Used with permission.

March 24: Ven. Fulton J. Sheen, *The World's First Love*, 83-84. Used with permission.

March 25: Pope Benedict XVI, *Deus Caritas Est*, 12.

March 26: Ven. Fulton J. Sheen, *The World's First Love*, 37. Used with permission.

March 27: Bl. Michael Sopocko, *God is Mercy*, 53. Used with permission.

March 28: Ven. Pope Paul VI, *Marialis Cultus*, 19.

March 29: St. Pope John XXIII, "Epistle to Cardinal Agaganian," (Jan. 31, 1959).

March 30: St. Faustina Kowalska, *Diary: Divine Mercy in My Soul*. (Stockbridge,MA: Marian Press, 2002), no. 1746. Used with permission.

March 31: Bl. Michael Sopocko, *God is Mercy*, 53. Used with permission.

April 1: St. John Damascene, PG 96, 744 C-D.

April 2: Ven. Pope Paul VI, *AAS 62: 300-301* (April 24, 1970).

April 3: Bl. James Alberione, *Glories and Virtues of Mary*. Trans. Hilda Calabro (Boston, MA: Daughters of St. Paul, 1982), 197.

April 4: St. Lawrence of Brindisi, as quoted in Arturo da Carmignano, O.F.M. Cap. *St. Lawrence of Brindisi*. Trans. Paul Barrett, O.F.M. Cap. (Westminster, MD: Newman Press, 1963), 129.

April 5: St. John Eudes, *The Admirable Heart of Mary*, 141.

April 6: Servant of God Frank Duff, "Everyone must pour himself into another soul," (1956), as quoted at www.catholicpamphlets.net

April 7: St. Maximilian Kolbe, as quoted in Fr. Stefano M. Manelli, F.I., *Devotion to Our Lady: The Marian Life as Taught by the Saints* (New Bedford, MA: Academy of the Immaculate, 2001), 15.

April 8: Bl. James Alberione, *Mary, Queen of the Apostles* (Derby, NY: Daughters of St. Paul, 1956), 33.

REFERENCES

April 9: Ven. Fulton J. Sheen, *Three to Get Married*, 163-164. Used with permission.

April 10: St. Louis de Montfort, *True Devotion*, 112. Used with permission.

April 11: St. Gemma Galgani, as quoted in Fr. Stefano Manelli, F.I. "Marian Coredemption in the Hagiography of the 20th Century," in *Mary at the Foot of the Cross: Acts of the International Symposium on Marian Coredemption* (New Bedford, MA: Academy of the Immaculate, 2001), 179.

April 12: St. John Paul II, *Dives in Misericordia*, 30.

April 13: Servant of God (Fr.) Joseph Kentenich, *Mary, Our Mother and Educator*, 129. Used with permission.

April 14: St. John Eudes, *The Admirable Heart of Mary*, 137.

April 15: St. John Paul II, *Dives in Misericordia*, 30.

April 16: St. Bernadette Soubirous, as quoted in Patricia A. McEachern, *A Holy Life: St. Bernadette of Lourdes* (San Francisco: Ignatius Press, 2005), 18-19.

April 17: St. John Eudes, *The Admirable Heart of Mary*, 127.

April 18: Bl. Ildefonso Schuster, as quoted in *Magnificat* (Vol. 14, No.3/May 2012), 65.

April 19: Bl. James Alberione, in Manelli "Marian Coredemption," 225.

April 20: St. Bernard of Clairvaux, in Eudes, *The Admirable Heart of Mary*, 127.

April 21: St. Anselm of Canterbury, PL 158, 451 A.

April 22: Ven. Fulton J. Sheen, *The World's First Love*, 73-74. Used with permission.

April 23: St. Anselm of Canterbury, PL 158, 956 B – 957 A.

April 24: St. Mary Euphrasia Pelletier, in *Magnificat* (Vol. 14, No.8/October 2012), 169.

April 25: St. Bernard of Clairvaux, PL 183, 441 C.

April 26: St. Gregory Palamas, PG 151, 469-470.

April 27: St. Peter Canisius, in Fehrenbach, *Mary, Day By Day*, 16.

April 28: St. Louis de Montfort, *True Devotion*, 59. Used with permission.

April 29: St. Catherine of Siena, *Dialogue of St. Catherine of Siena* (paragraph 139), in St. Alphonsus de Liguori, *The Glories of Mary* (Brooklyn: Redemptorist Fathers, 1931), 204 (Chapter VI, Section III).

April 30: Servant of God (Fr.) Joseph Kentenich, *Marian Instrument Piety*, 155. Used with permission.

May 1: Pope Benedict XVI (Joseph Cardinal Ratzinger) & Hans Urs von Balthasar, *Mary: The Church at the Source*. Trans. Adrian Walker (San Francisco: Ignatius Press, 2005), 88.

May 2: Ven. Fulton J. Sheen, *The World's First Love*, 20. Used with permission.

May 3: Pope Innocent III, in Moran, 63.

May 4: Servant of God (Fr.) Joseph Kentenich, *Mary, Our Mother and Educator*, 57. Used with permission.

May 5: Ven. Pope Paul VI, "To Marian Congregations," (Sept. 12, 1963).

May 6: Pope Benedict XVI, "*Angelus* message," (June 11, 2006).

May 7: Bl. James Alberione, *Mary, Hope of the World*, 10.

May 8: Servant of God Frank Duff, as quoted at www.legionofmary.ie.

May 9: Pope St. Pius X, in Nugent, 53. Used with permission.

May 10: Ven. Fulton J. Sheen, *The World's First Love*, 15. Used with permission.

May 11: St. Odilo of Cluny, PL 142, 915-916.

May 12: St. Germanus of Constantinople, PG 98, 380 B.

May 13: Servant of God (Fr.) Joseph Kentenich, *Mary, Our Mother and Educator*, 24-25. Used with permission.

May 14: Ven. Fulton J. Sheen, as quoted in Jason Evert, *Purity 365: Daily Reflections on True Love* (Cincinnati, OH: Servant Books, 2009), 53.

May 15: St. Anselm of Canterbury, PL 158, 957 A.

May 16: St. Lawrence of Brindisi, *Mariale*, 123.

May 17: Ven. Fulton J. Sheen, *The World's First Love*, 103. Used with permission.

May 18: Bl. Stanislaus Papczynski, *Templum Dei Mysticum*. Fontes Historiae Marianorum 5. (Varsaviae: Institutum Historicum Marianorum, 1998), 81.

May 19: St. Lawrence of Brindisi, *Mariale*, 382.

May 20: St. Bernardine of Siena, in Pope St. Pius X, *Ad diem illum laetissimum*, 13.

May 21: St. John Paul II, "General Audience," (December 6, 1995).

May 22: St. Teresa Benedicta of the Cross, *Writings of Edith Stein* (London: P. Owen, 1956), 170.

May 23: Pope Benedict XVI, "Homily at Mass for the Fifth World Meeting of Families," (July 9, 2006).

May 24: St. Raphaela Maria, in Chervin, 101.

May 25: Pope St. Gregory VII, PL 148, 327A.

May 26: St. Philip Neri, in *Magnificat* (Vol. 14, No.3/May 2012), 355.

May 27: St. John Eudes, *Kingdom of Jesus* (Part VI, Chapter XI), as quoted at www.piercedhearts.org.

May 28: St. Francis de Sales, *Introduction to the Devout Life*. Trans. John K. Ryan (New York: Doubleday, 2003), 96.

May 29: Servant of God (Fr.) Joseph Kentenich, *Marian Instrument Piety*, 153. Used with permission.

May 30: Pope Benedict XVI, "Address at Heiligenkreuz Abbey, Austria," (September 9, 2007).

May 31: Luke 1:48 (RSVCE).

June 1: Pope Benedict XVI, *Mary: The Church at the Source*, 62.

June 2: Bl. Michael Sopocko, *God is Mercy*, 52. Used with permission.

June 3: Ven. Pope Paul VI, "General Audience," (May 30, 1973).

June 4: Servant of God (Fr.) Joseph Kentenich, *Mary, Our Mother and Educator*, 105. Used with permission.

June 5: St. Bonaventure, as quoted in Fr. Patrick Greenough, O.F.M., Conv. *The Immaculate Conception and Other Teachings on the Blessed Virgin Mary* (Libertyville, IL: Marytown Press, 2005), 101.

June 6: Bl. George Matulaitis, *Journal*. Fontes Historiae Marianorum 17. Trans. Sr. Ann Mikaila, MVS (Stockbridge, MA: Marian Fathers, 2003), 138. Used with permission.

June 7: St. Maximilian Kolbe, *Maria Was His Middle Name*, 133.

June 8: St. John Vianney, *Thoughts of the Cure D'ars*. (Charlotte, NC: Tan Books, 1984), 33.

June 9: St. Ephrem the Syrian, as quoted in Sebastian Brock, *The Luminous Eye: The Spiritual World Vision of Saint Ephrem the Syrian*. (Kalamazoo, MI: Cistercian Publications, 1992), 127.

June 10: St. Cyril of Alexandria, in *Magnificat* (Vol. 14, No.10/December 2012), 302.

June 11: St. Augustine of Hippo, as quoted in Fr. Paul Segneri, S.J., *The Devout Client of Mary: Instructed in the Motives and Means of Serving Her Well*. (London: Burns & Lambert, 1857), 32.

June 12: St. Anthony Mary Claret, in Adels, 18.

June 13: St. Anthony of Padua, in *Magnificat* (Vol. 14, No.10/December 2012), 433.

June 14: Ven. Fulton J. Sheen, *The Rainbow of Sorrow*. (Garden City, NY: Garden City Books, 1953), 40.

June 15: St. Madeleine Sophie Barat, in Johnston, 138.

June 16: St. Lawrence of Brindisi, *Mariale*, 534.

June 17: St. John Eudes, *The Wondrous Childhood*, 132.

June 18: St. Padre Pio, *Padre Pio parla della Madonna*, as quoted in Fr. Stefano M. Manelli, F.I., *The Marian Vow* (New Bedford, MA: Academy of the Immaculate, 2010), 133.

June 19: Ven. Fulton J. Sheen, *The Priest Is Not His Own*. (New York: McGraw-Hill Book Company, Inc., 1963), 271-272.

June 20: Pope Benedict XVI, *God and the World: A Conversation with Peter Seewald* (San Francisco, CA: Ignatius Press, 2002), 302.

June 21: Servant of God Mother Auxilia de la Cruz, *The Eucharistic Life*, 68.

June 22: St. John Fisher, *Exposition of the Seven Penitential Psalms*, in modern English with an introduction by Anne Barbeau Gardiner (San Francisco: Ignatius Press, 1998), 55.

June 23: St. Joseph Cafasso, in Alberione, *Mary, Queen of the Apostles*, 319.

June 24: St. John Vianney, in Fehrenbach, *Mary, Day By Day*, 8.

June 25: St. Bernadette Soubirous, in Adels, 18.

June 26: St. Josemaria Escriva, *The Way: Furrow: The Forge*. (New York: Scepter, 2001), 123.

June 27: St. Cyril of Alexandria, PG 77, 992-996.

June 28: St. Irenaeus of Lyons, PG 7, 959-960.

June 29: St. Lawrence of Brindisi, *Mariale*, 307.

June 30: Ven. Mary of Agreda, in Moran, 169.

July 1: St. John Vianney, *Thoughts of the Cure D'ars*, 74.

July 2: Ven. Fulton J. Sheen, *The World's First Love*, 171. Used with permission.

July 3: St. Catherine of Siena, as quoted in J.M. Perrin, O.P., *Catherine of Siena*. Trans. Paul Barrett, O.F.M. Cap. (Westminster, MD: Newman Press, 1965), 186.

July 4: St. Andrew of Crete, in Ligouri, *The Glories of Mary* (Brooklyn, NY: Redemptorist Fathers, 1931), 85.

July 5: Ven. Pope Pius XII, "Allocution to Catholic Relief Services," Dec. 8, 1955.

July 6: Pope Leo XIII, *Magnae Dei Matris*, as quoted in W. Lawler, O.P., (ed.) *The Rosary of Mary: Translation of the Encyclicals and Apostolic Letters of Pope Leo XIII* (Paterson, NJ: 1944): 87-88.

July 7: St. John Vianney, in Fehrenbach, *Mary, Day By Day*, 161.

July 8: Pope Benedict XVI, "*Angelus* message," (December 8, 2005).

July 9: St. Veronica Giuliani, as quoted in Mother Francesca Perillo, F.I., "Marian Coredemption in St. Veronica Giuliani," *Mary at the Foot of the Cross: Acts of the*

REFERENCES

International Symposium on Marian Coredemption (New Bedford: Academy of the Immaculate, 2001), 246.

July 10: Bl. James Alberione, *Mary, Queen of the Apostles*, 250.

July 11: Servant of God (Fr.) Patrick J. Peyton, *The Ear of God* (New York: Doubleday & Company, Inc., 1951), 82.

July 12: St. Lawrence of Brindisi, *Mariale*, 369.

July 13: Servant of God (Fr.) Joseph Kentenich, *Marian Instrument Piety*, 39. Used with permission.

July 14: St. Maximilian Kolbe, in Manelli, *The Marian Vow*, 65.

July 15: St. Bonaventure, in Manelli, *Devotion to Our Lady*, 28.

July 16: Ven. Pope Pius XII, "Letter *Neminem profecto*," (February 11, 1950).

July 17: St. Peter Damian, PL 144, 740-748.

July 18: Servant of God (Fr.) Joseph Kentenich, *Marian Instrument Piety*, 142. Used with permission.

July 19: Ven. Fulton J. Sheen, *The World's First Love*, 85. Used with permission.

July 20: St. Thomas Aquinas, in Nugent, 1. Used with permission.

July 21: St. Lawrence of Brindisi, *Mariale*, 175.

July 22: St. Louis de Montfort, *True Devotion*, 12. Used with permission.

July 23: St. Bridget of Sweden, as quoted in John Cook, *The Book of Positive Quotations.* 2nd Edition. (Minneapolis: Fairview Press, 2007), 189.

July 24: St. Maximilian Kolbe, in Manelli, *The Marian Vow*, 111.

July 25: Servant of God (Fr.) Joseph Kentenich, *Marian Instrument Piety*, 152. Used with permission.

July 26: St. Ephrem the Syrian, *Oratio ad Santissimam Dei Matrem*, in *Enchiridion Marianum Biblicum Patristicum*. D. Casagrande (ed.) Rome: "Cor Unum" 1974, 346.

July 27: St. John Eudes, *The Wondrous Childhood*, 239.

July 28: Bl. William Joseph Chaminade, *From A Full Heart,* entry for Sept. 5.

July 29: St. Maximilian Kolbe, *Scritti di Massimiliano Kolbe* (Rome: Editrice Nazionale Milizia dell'Immacolata, 1997), 1334.

July 30: St. Peter Chrysologus, PL 52, 577.

July 31: Bl. William Joseph Chaminade, *From A Full Heart*, entry for Jan. 2.

August 1: St. Alphonsus Ligouri, as quoted in Bonaventure Hammer, O.F.M., *Mary, Help of Christians and the Fourteen Saints Invoked as Holy Helpers* (New York: Benziger Brothers, 1909), 362.

August 2: St. Peter Julian Eymard, *Our Lady of the Blessed Sacrament: Readings for the Month of May* (Cleveland, OH: Emmanuel Publications, 1930), 142.

August 3: St. John Eudes, *The Admirable Heart*, 201.

August 4: St. John Vianney, as quoted in Abbe Francois Trochu, *The Cure d'Ars: Saint Jean-Marie-Baptiste Vianney*. Trans. Dom Ernest Graf, O.S.B. (Rockford, IL: Tan Books, 1977), 8.

August 5: Bl. James Alberione, *Glories and Virtues of Mary*, 237.

August 6: St. Francis of Assisi, *The Office of the Passion*, as quoted in Marion A. Habig (ed.), *St. Francis of Assisi, Writings and Early Biographies: English Omnibus of the Sources* for the Life of St. Francis (Chicago, 1983), 142.

August 7: Ven. Mary of Agreda, *City of God: The Conception: The Divine History and Life of the Virgin Mother of God*. Trans. Fiscar Marison. (Washington, NJ: Ave Maria Institute, 1971), 220.

August 8: Ven. Fulton J. Sheen, *The World's First Love*, 171. Used with permission.

August 9: St. Teresa Benedicta of the Cross, in Evert, *Purity*, 365, 82.

August 10: St. John Eudes, *The Wondrous Childhood*, 99-100.

August 11: Bl. Gabriel Maria Allegra, *Mary's Immaculate Heart: A Way to God*. Trans. Joachim Daleiden, O.F.M. (Chicago: Franciscan Herald Press, 1985), 22.

August 12: St. John Paul II, in Evert, *Purity*, 365, 86.

August 13: St. Germanus of Constantinople, in Pope Leo XIII *Adiutricem*, 14.

August 14: St. Maximilian Kolbe, as quoted in Fr. Angelo M. Geiger, F.I., "Marian Mediation as Presence and Transubstantiation into the Immaculate," in *Mary at the Foot of the Cross III: Mater Unitatis: Acts of the Third International Symposium on Marian Coredemption* (New Bedford, MA: Academy of the Immaculate, 2003), 157-158.

August 15: Servant of God (Fr.) Joseph Kentenich, *Mary, Our Mother and Educator*, 104. Used with permission.

August 16: St. John Vianney, *Thoughts of the Cure D'ars*, 32.

August 17: Pope Benedict XVI, "Homily as Mass for the canonization of St. Anthony of St. Anne Galvao, Aparecida, Brazil," (May 11, 2007).

August 18: Pope Leo XIII, *Octobri Mense*, 4.

August 19: St. John Eudes, *The Admirable Heart*, 4.

August 20: St. Bernard of Clairvaux, as quoted in Bruce M. Metzger and Michael D. Coogan (ed.), *The Oxford Guide to Ideas & Issues of the Bible* (New York: Oxford University Press, 2001), 303.

REFERENCES

August 21: Pope St. Pius X, *Ad Diem Illum Laetissimum*, 6.

August 22: St. John Eudes, *The Wondrous Childhood*, 237.

August 23: St. Thomas of Villanova, *The Works of Saint Thomas of Villanova: Marian Sermons*. Trans. Daniel Hobbins & Matthew J. O'Connell. (Villanova, PA: Augustinian Press, 2001), 52. Used with permission.

August 24: Bl. Luigi Orione, in Manelli, "Marian Coredemption," 209.

August 25: Servant of God (Fr.) Joseph Kentenich, *Marian Instrument Piety*, 166. Used with permission.

August 26: St. John Damascene, in Adels, 21.

August 27: St. Maximilian Kolbe, as quoted in H.M. Manteau-Bonamy, O.P., *Immaculate Conception and the Holy Spirit: The Marian Teachings of St. Maximilian Kolbe*. Trans. Richard Arnandez, FSC (Libertyville, IL: Franciscan Marytown Press, 1977), 108.

August 28: St. Augustine of Hippo, in Moran, 32.

August 29: St. Louis de Montfort, *True Devotion*, 114. Used with permission.

August 30: Bl. Ildefonso Schuster, in *Magnificat* (Vol. 14, No.8/October 2012), 290.

August 31: Servant of God Catherine de Hueck Doherty, as quoted in *The Air We Breathe: The Mariology of Catherine de Hueck Doherty* by Fr. Denis Raymond Lemieux. (New Bedford, MA: Academy of the Immaculate, 2011), 77.

September 1: Servant of God (Fr.) Joseph Kentenich, *Mary, Our Mother and Educator*, 122. Used with permission.

September 2: St. Vincent Pallotti, in Kentenich, *Mary, Our Mother and Educator*, 176. Used with permission.

September 3: St. Bernardine of Siena, in Adels, 20.

September 4: Bl. Dina Belanger, *The Autobiography of Dina Belanger*. Trans. Mary St. Stephen, R.J.M. (Canada: Religious of Jesus and Mary, 1997), 64-65.

September 5: Bl. Teresa of Calcutta, *Letter to Vox Populi Mariae Mediatrici*, August 14, 1993, Vox Populi Mariae Mediatrici Archives. Hopedale, Ohio.

September 6: St. Phillip Neri, in Adels, 18.

September 7: St. Lawrence of Brindisi, *Mariale*, 449-450.

September 8: St. Peter Julian Eymard, *Our Lady of the Blessed Sacrament*, 31.

September 9: St. Thomas of Villanova, *Marian Sermons*. 108. Used with permission.

September 10: St. John Damascene, PG 94, 1029-1030.

September 11: St. Bonaventure, in Ligouri, *The Glories of Mary*, 122-123.

September 12: St. Bonaventure, in Adels, 18.

September 13: St. John Paul II, "Homily of Pope John Paul II at Fatima," (May 13, 1982).

September 14: Ven. Pope Paul VI, "Sermon in the parish church of Castel Gandolfo" (Aug. 15, 1964)

September 15: Servant of God (Fr.) Joseph Kentenich, *Mary, Our Mother and Educator*, 19. Used with permission.

September 16: St. Anselm of Canterbury, PL 158, 951 B.

September 17: St. Robert Bellarmine, in Fehrenbach, *Mary, Day By Day*, 136.

September 18: Pope Pius XI, *Allocution to Pilgrims from Vicenza*, as quoted in Msgr. Arthur Burton Calkins, "Mary Co-Redemptrix: The Beloved Associate of Christ" in *Mariology: A Guide for Priests, Deacons, Seminarians, and Consecrated Persons* (Goleta, CA: Queenship Publishing, 2007), 378.

September 19: Ven. Fulton J. Sheen, *The World's First Love*, 266. Used with permission.

September 20: Ven. Bernard Maria Clausi, as quoted in Fr. Paul Maria Sigl "The Spiritual Maternity of Mary in the Lives of the Saints," in *Mary at the Foot of the Cross V: Redemption and Coredemption under the Sign of the Immaculate Conception: Acts of the International Symposium on Marian Coredemption* (New Bedford, MA: Academy of the Immaculate, 2005), 553.

September 21: St. John Damascene, PG 94, 1161.

September 22: St. Thomas of Villanova, *Marian Sermons*, 63. Used with permission.

September 23: St. Padre Pio, *Padre Pio's Words of Hope*. Ed. Eileen Dunn Bertanzetti (Huntington, IN: Our Sunday Visitor, Inc., 1999), 117.

September 24: St. John Eudes, *The Admirable Heart*, 169.

September 25: Servant of God (Fr.) Joseph Kentenich, *Marian Instrument Piety*, 138. Used with permission.

September 26: Bl. John Henry Newman, *Mary: The Virgin Mary in the Life and Writings of John Henry Newman*. (ed.) Philip Boyce (Leominster, Herefordshire: Gracewing Publishing, 2001), 344.

September 27: St. Proclus of Constantinople, in Adels, 21.

September 28: Servant of God (Fr.) Joseph Kentenich, *Marian Instrument Piety*, 136. Used with permission.

REFERENCES

September 29: Bl. Pope Pius IX, *Ineffabilis Deus*, 17.

September 30: St. Lawrence of Brindisi, *Mariale*, 131.

October 1: Thérèse of Lisieux, as quoted in Charles P. Connor, *The Saint for the Third Millennium: St. Therese of Lisieux* (New York: Alba House, 2007), 164. Used with permission.

October 2: St. Ambrose Autpert, PL 39, 2131.

October 3: Bl. Columba Marmion, *Christ the Life of the Soul* (Bethesda, MD: Zaccheus Press, 2005), 385.

October 4: St. Francis of Assisi, as quoted in Fr. Peter Damian M. Fehlner, F.I., "Virgo Ecclesia Facta: The Immaculate Conception, St. Francis of Assisi, and the Renewal of the Church," in *The Immaculate Conception in the Life of the Church: Essays from the International Mariological Symposium in Honor of the 150th Anniversary of the Proclamation of the Dogma of the Immaculate Conception.* (ed.) Donald H. Calloway, M.I.C. (Stockbridge, MA: Marian Press, 2004), 84. Used with permission.

October 5: St. Faustina Kowalska, *Diary*, no. 79. Used with permission.

October 6: Bl. Bartolo Longo, in St. John Paul II, *Rosarium Virginis Mariae*, 43.

October 7: Bl. Pope Pius IX, as quoted in *The Official Handbook of the Legion of Mary.* (Dublin: Concilium Legionis Mariae, 2005), 146.

October 8: St. Louis de Montfort, *The Secret of the Rosary.* Trans. Mary Barbour, T.O.P. (Bay Shore, NY: Montfort Publications, 1954), 91. Used with permission.

October 9: Bl. John Henry Newman, Discourses, as quoted in Michael O'Carroll, C.S.Sp., *Theotokos: A Theological Encyclopedia of the Blessed Virgin Mary* (Collegeville, MN: Liturgical Press, 1982), 264.

October 10: Pope Leo XIII, *Adiutricem*, 4.

October 11: St. Pope John XXIII, as quoted in Andrew J. Gerakas, *The Rosary and Devotion to Mary* (Boston, MA: St. Paul Books & Media, 1992), 23.

October 12: St. Louis de Montfort, *The Secret of the Rosary*, 61. Used with permission.

October 13: Servant of God (Fr.) Joseph Kentenich, *Marian Instrument Piety*, 77. Used with permission.

October 14: St. John Paul II, *Rosarium Virginis Mariae*, 5.

October 15: Ven. Fulton J. Sheen, in Nugent, 55. Used with permission.

October 16: St. John Vianney, *Thoughts of the Cure D'ars*, 59.

October 17: Bl. Timothy Giaccardo, as quoted in *Spiritual Advice from the Saints:*

365 Days of Inspiration. Compiled by Daughters of St. Paul (Boston: Pauline Books & Media, 2004), entry for October 7.

October 18: St. Francis de Sales, in *Magnificat* (Vol. 14, No.3/May 2012), 156.

October 19: Ven. Matt Talbot, as quoted in Mary Purcell, *Remembering Matt Talbot* (Dublin: M.H. Gill and Sons, Ltd., 1990), 38.

October 20: Ven. Fulton J. Sheen, *The World's First Love*, 13. Used with permission.

October 21: Ven. Casimir Wyszynski, as quoted in *Marian Prayers* (Rome-Stockbridge: Congregation of Marian Fathers, 2010), 18-19. Used with permission.

October 22: St. John Paul II, "Papal Address in Washington, D.C.," October 6, 1979.

October 23: St. Luigi Guanella, in *Magnificat* (Vol. 14, No.3 /May 2012), 44.

October 24: St. Anthony Mary Claret, in Ball, 65.

October 25: St. Pope John XXIII, as quoted in Pope Paul VI, *Mary, God's Mother and Ours* (Boston, MA: Daughters of St. Paul, 1979), 14.

October 26: St. Bernard of Clairvaux, PL 183, 441 B.

October 27: St. John Paul II, *Letter to Women* (June 29, 1995).

October 28: Ven. Fulton J. Sheen, *The World's First Love*, 171. Used with permission.

October 29: St. Alphonsus Liguori, *Hail Holy Queen! An Explanation of the 'Salve Regina' and the Role of the Blessed Mother in our Salvation* (Rockford, IL: Tan Books, 1995), 18-19.

October 30: Ven. Casimir Wyszynski, as quoted in Zygmunt Proczek, M.I.C., *The Servant of Mary Immaculate: Father Casimir Wyszynski* (Stockbridge, MA: Marians of the Immaculate Conception, 1997), 71. Used with permission.

October 31: St. Maximilian Kolbe, *Maria Was His Middle Name*, 72.

November 1: St. Louis de Montfort, *True Devotion*, 19. Used with permission.

November 2: St. John Eudes, *The Wondrous Childhood*, 286.

November 3: Pope Benedict XVI , Mary: *The Church at the Source*, 66.

November 4: Ven. Fulton J. Sheen, *The World's First Love*, 83. Used with permission.

November 5: St. Amadeus of Lausanne, as quoted in Michael O'Carroll, C.S.Sp., *Theotokos: A Theological Encyclopedia of the Blessed Virgin Mary* (Collegeville, MN: Liturgical Press, 1982), 15.

November 6: Bl. Isaac of Stella, PL 194, 1862-1863.

November 7: Pope Benedict XVI, Mary: *The Church at the Source*, 16-17.

November 8: Bl. John Duns Scotus, as quoted in Fr. Stefano M. Manelli, F.I., *Blessed*

REFERENCES

John Duns Scotus: Marian Doctor (New Bedford, MA: Academy of the Immaculate, 2011), 88.

November 9: St. Augustine of Hippo, in Nugent, 20. Used with permission.

November 10: St. Leo the Great, PL 54, 206.

November 11: Ven. Pope Pius XII, Mystici Corporis, 111.

November 12: St. Ephrem the Syrian, in Gambero, *Mary and the Fathers of the Church*, 115.

November 13: St. Ambrose, in Adels, 20.

November 14: St. Gregory Palamas, PG 151, 177B.

November 15: St. Albert the Great, *De Natura Boni*, 59, as quoted in Michael O'Carroll, C.S.Sp., *Theotokos: A Theological Encyclopedia of the Blessed Virgin Mary* (Collegeville, MN: Liturgical Press, 1982), 11.

November 16: Servant of God Mother Auxilia de la Cruz, *The Eucharistic Life*, 68.

November 17: St. Lawrence of Brindisi, *Mariale*, 39.

November 18: Servant of God (Fr.) Joseph Kentenich, *Marian Instrument Piety*, 127. Used with permission.

November 19: St. Thomas of Villanova, *Marian Sermons*, 117. Used with permission.

November 20: St. Proclus of Constantinople, PG 65, 717 C – 720 A.

November 21: St. Lawrence of Brindisi, *Mariale*, 187.

November 22: St. John Paul II, *Mulieris Dignitatem*, 22.

November 23: Pope Benedict XVI, Mary: *The Church at the Source*, 59-60.

November 24: St. Alphonsus Ligouri, *The Glories of Mary*, 85-86.

November 25: St. Leonard of Port Maurice, in Greenough, 104.

November 26: Bl. James Alberione, *Glories and Virtues of Mary*, 18.

November 27: St. Francis Anthony Fasani, in Greenough, 104.

November 28: St. Lawrence of Brindisi, *Mariale*, 172.

November 29: Pope Benedict XVI, "Homily at First Vespers, Solemnity of Mary, Mother of God," (December 31, 2007).

November 30: St. Catherine of Siena, as quoted in J.M. Perrin, O.P., *Catherine of Siena*. Trans. Paul Barrett, O.F.M. Cap. (Westminster, MD: Newman Press, 1965), 185.

December 1: Pope Benedict XVI, *Mary: The Church at the Source*, 46-47.

December 2: St. Anthony of Padua, in Gambero, *Mary in the Middle Ages*, 204.

December 3: St. Maximilian Kolbe, in Adels, 18.

December 4: St. John Damascene, PG 96, 753 B-C.

December 5: St. Faustina Kowalska, *Diary*, no. 1413. Used with permission.

December 6: Bl. Michael Sopocko, *The Mercy of God*, 78.

December 7: Bl. George Matulaitis, *Journal*. Fontes Historiae Marianorum 17. Trans. Sr. Ann Mikaila, MVS (Stockbridge, MA: Marian Fathers, 2003), 60. Used with permission.

December 8: Bl. Stanislaus Papczynski, as quoted in Tadeusz Rogalewski, M.I.C., *Stanislaus Papczynski (1631-1701): Founder of the Order of Marians and Inspirer of the Marian School of Spirituality*. Trans. Paul & Ewa St. Jean (Stockbridge, MA: Marian Press, 2001), 255. Used with permission.

December 9: St. Maximilian Kolbe, in Manelli, *Devotion to Our Lady*, 53.

December 10: St. John Paul II, "Angelus Message," December 8, 2003.

December 11: St. John Paul II, "Message to Cardinal Javier Lozano Barragan," February 11, 2004.

December 12: Our Lady's words to St. Juan Diego, as quoted in *A Handbook on Guadalupe* (New Bedford, MA: Academy of the Immaculate, 1997), 200.

December 13: Ven. Pope Pius XII, in Manelli, *Devotion to Mary*, 50.

December 14: St. John Paul II, *Rosarium Virginis Mariae*, 14.

December 15: St. Augustine of Hippo, in Gambero, *Mary and the Fathers of the Church*, 224.

December 16: St. John Eudes, *The Wondrous Childhood*, 214.

December 17: Servant of God (Fr.) Patrick J. Peyton, *Father Peyton's Rosary Prayer Book* (San Francisco, CA: Ignatius Press, 2003), 230.

December 18: St. Thomas of Villanova, *Marian Sermons*, 222. Used with permission.

December 19: St. Peter Damian, as quoted in Deyanira Flores, "Virgin Mother of Christ: Mary, The Church, and the Faithful Soul: Patristic and Medieval Testimonies on This Inseparable Trio." *Marian Studies*, Vol. LVII (2006), 101.

December 20: St. Josemaria Escriva, *Friends of God* (Manila: Sinag-tala, 2000), Chapter 17, No. 276.

December 21: St. John Paul II, *Ecclesia de Eucharistia*, 55.

December 22: St. Proclus of Constantinople, PG 65, 684 B.

December 23: Ven. Fulton J. Sheen, *Three to Get Married*, 161. Used with permission.

December 24: Pope St. Pius X, *Ad Diem Illum Laetissimum*, 15.

REFERENCES

December 25: Ven. Fulton J. Sheen, *Moods and Truths.* (Garden City, NY: Garden City Books, 1950), 100-101.

December 26: Servant of God Mother Auxilia de la Cruz, *Broken Bread.* Trans. Leonard P. Fitzpatrick, M.Ss.A. (Stockbridge, MA: Marian Helpers, 1983), 49. Used with permission.

December 27: St. John Paul II, "General Audience," May 11, 1983

December 28: St. Lawrence of Brindisi, *Mariale*, 243.

December 29: St. Peter Julian Eymard, *Our Lady of the Blessed Sacrament*, 68-69.

December 30: Servant of God Mother Auxilia de la Cruz, *Broken Bread*, 49. Used with permission.

December 31: Ven. Fulton J. Sheen, *The World's First Love*, 75-76. Used with permission.

Reflections

About the Author

Fr. Donald Calloway, MIC, a convert to Catholicism, is a member of the Congregation of Marians of the Immaculate Conception. Before his conversion to Catholicism, he was a high school dropout who had been kicked out of a foreign country, institutionalized twice, and thrown in jail multiple times. After his radical conversion, he earned a B.A. in Philosophy and Theology from the Franciscan University of Steubenville, Ohio, M.Div. and S.T.B. degrees from the Dominican House of Studies in Washington, D.C., and an S.T.L. in Mariology from the International Marian Research Institute in Dayton, Ohio. In addition to *Under the Mantle: Marian Thoughts from a 21st Century Priest,* he has written *No Turning Back: A Witness to Mercy*, a bestseller that recounts his dramatic conversion story (Marian Press 2010). He also is the author of the book *Purest of All Lilies: The Virgin Mary in the Spirituality of St. Faustina* (Marian Press, 2008). Further, he has written many academic articles and is the editor of two books: *The Immaculate Conception in the Life of the Church* (Marian Press, 2004) and *The Virgin Mary and Theology of the Body* (Marian Press, 2005).

Fr. Calloway is the Vicar Provincial for the Mother of Mercy Province and the Vocation Director for the Marians.

To learn more about Marian vocations, visit
www.marian.org/vocations
or visit
Fr. Calloway's website,
www.fathercalloway.com

 Find Fr. Calloway on Facebook

facebook.com/donald.calloway.5

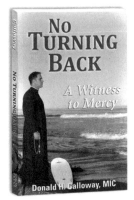

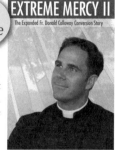
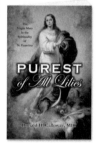
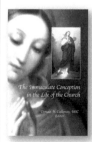
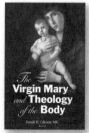

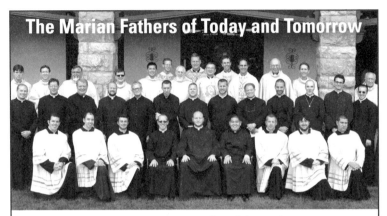

THIRTEENTH
OF THE MONTH CLUB

Fr. Donald Calloway, MIC,
Marian Vocation Director,
will participate in a recurring
feature in the Thirteenth of
the Month Club newsletter.

I'm honored and delighted to do this for the club, since it's a good way for me to help people come to a better place in their relationship with Our Lady. I want to let people know that by being in the Thirteenth of the Month Club, they're part of the Marian family. They are praying for us [the Marian Fathers of the Immaculate Conception], and we are praying for them.

13th of the Month Club members are a group of special friends who help support the work of the Marians of the Immaculate Conception. On the 13th of each month, members pray the Rosary for the intentions of the Club. The Marians residing in Fatima offer a special Mass on the 13th of the month for members' intentions. All members pledge a monthly gift and receive the Club newsletter published by the Association of Marian Helpers, Stockbridge, MA 01263.

For more information:
Call: 1-800-671-2020   Online: www.marian.org
E-mail: thirteenth@marian.org